# Looking Forward to Monday Morning
## A Residential Architect's Compendium
by
## Daniel Frisch, AIA

*Essays, Observations, Dispatches*

EDITIONS

ORO Editions
Publishers of Architecture, Art, and Design
Gordon Goff: Publisher

www.oroeditions.com
info@oroeditions.com

Published by ORO Editions

Author: Daniel Frisch
Book Design: James H. Schriebl
Project Manager: Jake Anderson

10 9 8 7 6 5 4 3 2 1 First Edition

ISBN: 978-1-961856-49-3

**Prepress and Print work by ORO Editions Inc.**
**Printed in China**

ORO Editions makes a continuous effort to minimize the overall carbon footprint of its publications. As part of this goal, ORO, in association with Global ReLeaf, arranges to plant trees to replace those used in the manufacturing of the paper produced for its books. Global ReLeaf is an international campaign run by American Forests, one of the world's oldest nonprofit conservation organizations. Global ReLeaf is American Forests' education and action program that helps individuals, organizations, agencies, and corporations improve the local and global environment by planting and caring for trees.

To my parents Nelle and Don Frisch, who set the bar high.

To my wife Darcy and children Nelle and Buddy,
who inspire me to be my very best.

To every member of the DFA team—now and through the years,
for patiently enduring so many Monday Morning Meetings
and for helping to get it right.

To every classmate, professor, colleague, client, consultant,
contractor, and collaborator for everything.

To my many, many friends, who together have made me
richer than George Bailey.

All of you have been, and continue to be, my teachers.
If my words ring true, please know I borrowed them from you.

*DF 2014*

# Contents

# INTRODUCTION

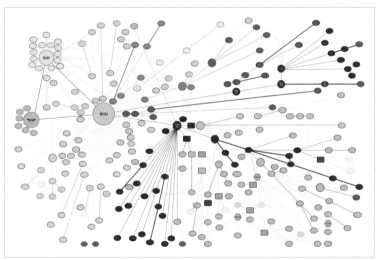

*DEA Client Graph - See "Bubble Chart," page 199*

# Looking Forward To Monday Morning

During the fall of 2016, I was strolling along one of Olmstead's Central Park paths with a fellow dad from our kids' school, and he said quite casually that I should write about my work. Although I had thought about it over the years, his remark gave me that little push to go out the next week and buy my first laptop. My initial efforts were introductory roadmaps for what I was going to write about and why. I was simply trying to explain and justify my project to myself, and looking back on the earliest pieces, it is very clear how much I didn't know. I didn't know how trying I would find writing to be or how proud I would feel when I finally came back to rewrite this "introduction."

I was born a year after the baby boom in Manhattan, the second child of two natural science academics. At six months and with me just emerging from the NICU, my father accepted a teaching position at Northwestern, and we moved from New York to Chicago. Six years later, it was on to Grand Rapids, Michigan, for an exciting but short-lived teaching and research position, followed by an equally short-lived early retirement. After a few years of selling real estate, my parents opened an independent bookstore in Grand Rapids, and after that closed (a long family tradition of passionate but questionable entrepreneurship), they wrote and published a farmers' market cookbook. I still reference the volume and occasionally search the internet for used copies in good condition. My parents have been gone for a while (father 1996, mother 2008), and while I miss them very much, I think they would have enjoyed watching me start a family of my own, nurture a firm, and finally, to welcome another writer to the family.

My formal studies in architecture began in the tenth grade at East Grand Rapids Senior High School where I took both shop and mechanical drawing classes. While I took typing but skipped home economics, it was our mechanical drawing teacher, Dan Graham, who lit the fuse. And, upon the recommendation of an artist friend of my parents, I applied to the summer 1982 Career Discovery Program at Harvard University. The acceptance letter was the first of a number of surprisingly affirmative responses to school applications. That summer I was the youngest student in an intensive six-week program at Harvard's Graduate School of Design (GSD), taking lecture, seminar, and studio classes—exactly as I would for seven years in architecture school.

Those seven years of architecture school were spent at the University of Virginia and Columbia University, with a one-year sabbatical between. At Virginia, I fell in love over and over again with architecture and design, demonstrably reinforcing the decision I had made to pursue my future in the field. After graduation, I moved to Manhattan and landed an intern position at a young firm, a training that was every bit as valuable and confirming as my studies. Graduate school at Columbia gave me useful insight into the competitiveness of the field; in the academy and in the profession, stiff spines and broad shoulders are required. I graduated in 1991 during a recessionary trough and was thrilled to get a job offer even before receiving my Statement of Arrears – my physical diploma would come ten years later. The only problem being that the job offer wasn't for a job, but more accurately, for an industry-norm internship. This one was for a "Starchitect" for whom I had been a teaching assistant during my last two years of graduate school. When I effusively thanked him for the offer, I also asked about some of the job particulars including hours and compensation. He seemed a bit taken aback, or possibly, insulted by the question. As for the number of hours I would be expected to "work," he referred me to his other apprentices, many of whom I knew, and who routinely logged eighty hours a week. As for compensation, the starting base salary was zero, to be adjusted at the principal's discretion at such time that my work product was a contribution to the firm. Wasn't I the fortunate one?

Six weeks after graduation, I tacked a different way and with two partners, started our firm. I was twenty-five years old and young enough not to know better and also certain there was a better model than the one I had otherwise considered. I could not have done this without my two partners, Edward Cabot, a friend and classmate from Columbia, and Amy Lesser, an architect and my first cousin. While the partnership didn't survive, I'll never forget the giddy enthusiasm we felt during the first years and know with the clarity of hindsight that I could not tell these stories without our shared belief and optimism.

When we founded the firm, our unwritten business plan was straightforward: meet clients, design their homes, and celebrate our success. Easy. Although I recall innumerable struggles and difficult decisions, most were reactive to circumstances, not the product of our planning or, more accurately, our lack of planning. For many years, I would start the week onerously writing in longhand on a yellow pad, a to-do list of everything needed to be done. The top of the list was dominated by items which were repeated every week yet were unlikely to be undertaken. While the endeavor took discipline and was proof, largely to self, of unwavering dedication, the exercise was much less productive than intended. The numbing repetition was not a predictor or celebration of success but the recording of the unaccomplished. Without knowing it, I had created a depressing and solitary way to start the week whose only salvation was saving others from writer's cramp. After a dozen or so years and with a great sense of relief, I abandoned the practice of Monday morning to-do lists.

In 2016 and with our practice flourishing, we committed to a long-range growth plan. We leased the floor above our townhouse home of twenty-two years and expanded the team to a headcount in the low double digits—and fingers crossed—we keep growing. Amongst the dust and upheaval of the expansion, we began holding Monday morning meetings. While nothing compares to the Quaker meeting with its prolonged silence, our meetings have become my personal bully pulpit. My Monday morning conversations with our team sometimes cover recent project developments, yet more often introduce broader concepts, addressing the "why" of what we do - a running conversation seemingly without limits. In the posts that follow, you will have a seat at our Monday morning table, enjoying a weekly discussion that always leaves me "Looking Forward to Monday Morning." There's no place I'd rather be.

# WARMING UP

*DF 1986*

# Little Ego : Big Ego

Stereotyping architects is easy. Beyond the superficial wire-rimmed glasses, black turtlenecks, and sport coats with elbow patches, architects are universally and fairly characterized as egotistical and arrogant. As a rule, we architects do little to discourage the stereotype. We dress the part, play along, and laugh at ourselves—all the while hanging on with pride as the imagery affords a certain distinction.

I suspect the apparent outsize ego of the architect is accurate, but also misunderstood. Fighting small battles, stubbornness, grandstanding, and winning arguments may all rather be signs of an undersized ego stemming from low self-esteem coupled with a fear of losing, or even worse, being wrong. Success in many disciplines derives from and fuels the ego, and in most disciplines, systems abound by which to measure success. Hollywood has the Academy Awards, and business has Forbes Magazine and its lists ranking the wealth of individuals and corporations. And sports, well, scorekeeping was invented to track and compare accomplishments.

Architecture and design, however, inhabit an alternative world of subjectivity, and especially so for residential practitioners. While Architectural Digest publishes and even ranks the most famous amongst us, most small firms toil anonymously, endeavoring to meet and exceed client expectations through quality design and competent project management. To succeed at this requires more than an average ego.

Excelling as a residential architect demands an ego so superior that the pressure to be always right and to win small battles drops away. To collaborate, to work in the service of others, and to rigorously solve problems requires the self-confidence to listen, to assess complex and often conflicting criteria, and to divine insightful answers without arrogance and self-interest.

Like most sermons, the foregoing sounds easy. Hard work, experience, and the constant pursuit of excellence are together the simplest prescription I know to attain confidence and to have one's ego grow from a stereotypical and superficially large ego into something greater.

**Introvert : Extrovert:**

One of my favorite aphorisms is that extroverts draw energy from engaging with others, whereas introverts find interactions with others draining.

If architecture is at the crossroads of art and science, then likewise, I believe for an architect to be successful, he or she must be both an introvert and an extrovert. I spend most of my days in exuberant extroversion, surrounded by people, and drawing energy from our community of friends, colleagues, clients, and contractors. Yet when working creatively, I find just as frequently a need to draw (pun intended) from within myself. Similarly, some members of our team are outgoing, others are guarded—and both personalities are welcome and essential. With our introverts, we work on their social skills; with our extroverts, we work on their focus and train their ability to tune out the din around them.

Several summers ago, we hosted a high school student intern from China. He only interned for a short while, and I can neither remember his name nor his strengths and weaknesses. And yet, I do vividly recall one specific exchange. On a subway ride back to the office after a site meeting, I asked if he had any questions for me. He pondered for a bit, and then said in a very quiet voice, "Mr. Frisch, do you have to talk so much to be an architect?" For a moment at least, I was at a loss for words.

# Hear, Hear

Several times I have looked up the expression "hear, hear...." Does the expression mean people in agreement are present (here), or that the speaker had been heard? Of course, it is the latter; a statement of agreement, just as "hear ye, hear ye..." is a call to attention. It took me a long time to equate "hear, hear..." with "yes, and...," and to recognize that while idioms change, groups of people have forever found ways to affirmatively communicate. A quick etymology search dates "hear, hear..." to the 17th century when parliamentarians would intone "hear him, hear him...;" thereafter shortened to simply "hear, hear...."

I first understood the power of listening by observing the unique qualities of a particularly popular high school friend. This teen had a lot going for him: he was capable on the pitch and rink, a captain of both the soccer and hockey teams, and he was smart and dressed well. While athletic accomplishment, intelligence, and vanity are undeniable predictors of social success, these traits were only partially responsible for my friend's popularity. He was quiet without being aloof, and after close observation, I realized he was a natural and sincere listener. Upon reflection, I am not sure which was more unique, the skills my friend exhibited or my competitive and jealous need to understand and emulate them.

Ever since figuring this out, I've tried to be a better listener. Listening doesn't always come as naturally to me as it seemed to for my classmate. By the time we were in high school together, I had learned many other adolescent lessons that conflicted with the patience necessary to be a great listener. Narcissism and a constant need to be the center of attention leap to mind. Self-awareness and leadership require some of these other traits, but they can only take one so far, and even set one back. Our greatest accomplishments often come through collaboration, which is facilitated by careful and sincere listening.

Listening takes practice, and sometimes we are gently reminded that other traits and priorities have impacted our hearing. By illustration, I recall the schematic design phase of a project featuring additions and renovations to a cherished National Historic Registry home owned by a repeat client. In consultation with a local architect, who was also the chair of the community's historic district commission, I proposed building the primary addition directly behind the main house, thereby using the historic home to shield the new addition. While this deference to the historic structure was thoughtful and nuanced, our client objected. The proposed additions turned the existing small living room into an appropriately scaled entry foyer, yet materially changed the feel of the home—specifically, the feel of the owner's favorite room. After a few presentations and false starts, I received a heartfelt and apologetic email from the client sharing, in spite of working together on a number of projects, that I simply was not listening. As architects and designers, we enjoy our share of criticism, but "not listening?" After receiving the email and having given it a tremendous amount of thought, we reconsidered the design approach, eventually going forward with a new design that simultaneously satisfied the client's program and respected the home's historic significance.

Those who know me well, and who struggle to get a word in edgewise when I get going, might be surprised by this treatise on listening. Working with my team and when writing these essays, I enjoy my bully pulpit and being the center of attention. Notwithstanding, it is possible that I can simultaneously care about empathy and collaboration and am sincere about practicing "yes, and…" In the words of yesteryear, "hear, hear…."

# The Small Firm Challenge

One of the most influential books on my shelf is *The Small Mart Revolution – How Local Businesses are Beating Global Competition* by Michael H. Schuman (2007). The concepts set forth by Schuman are not new, but in addition to his insightful socio-economic observations, he uses data to specifically encourage investment in our local communities by mathematically affirming the economic return to the community achieved by shopping local. Throughout the second half of the 20th century, Main Streets were under continuous siege, and the first decades of the twenty-first have seen this threat become more acute. A flight to the suburbs brought us the shopping mall, which in turn, fell from favor with the development of the big-box store. Whether we assess the impact of urban decay or the decline of the small town, our social structures are constantly being redefined. The suburban mall, Walmart, and Amazon have, without a doubt, streamlined and aided commerce, adding value by bringing goods to market with ever greater efficiency. The challenge, as I see it, is to adopt and adapt to each new paradigm, while fiercely fighting for the ongoing success of small businesses and the local community.

For years, advocates for Main Street have argued vocally and passionately for shopping locally and for supporting small businesses. Even American Express is in on it, with its Small Business Saturday and Shop Small programs (ironic though this may be for one of the thirty Dow Jones Industrial companies). We try to do our part, even with admittedly frequent Amazon deliveries, and we encourage friends and family to do the same. Our awareness and small contributions add up, I hope. We shop locally, we invest in solar, own an EV, and religiously recycle. While we are not full-blown hippies, we do endeavor to manage our environmental and economic resources in a manner that is net positive.

Digging a bit deeper, I realize these values comprise the core of our practice and help to answer the question "why?" Why have we chosen the path of establishing a small practice focusing on individual residential commissions? And, why does it matter – so much that we have become belligerently evangelical about the practice and its importance? Our schooling taught us to dream big, to rethink how people live, and how people relate to one another – spatially, environmentally, socially, and globally. As graduates, we alit upon the world with our diplomas, trained to be big-thinking leaders solving the world's largest problems. Yet, I opted instead to maintain a low profile, running a small firm with a non-exploitive culture, and with a core mission of client service. When I think of the businesses I admire, they are invariably closely held local businesses with long-term loyal employees. These are the stores in which I shop and the restaurants in which I eat. It's true, too, of the consultants with whom we work. Our engineers, expeditors, accountants, lawyers, and, most especially, our contracting partners are all small businesses we consider extensions of our family.

Unto itself, our office culture explains and ensures the vitality of the firm and validates its significance. Of equal motivation is our commitment to old-fashioned client service and making a difference. While DFA is not the largest, most profitable, or best-known architectural firm, I believe we are first when it comes to client satisfaction and with respect to the positive impact we have upon the lives of our clients. As embarrassing as it may feel, I've been told by a number of clients how affirmatively transformative our work has been upon their daily lives.

Making a difference matters, even more than profitability. Years after we finish a project, we are thrilled when we hear from former clients, whether they are experiencing problems for which we can lend a hand, or because they are contemplating a new project. Our clients have become our friends and our friends have become our clients. This may be confusing to some, as many are trained to separate 'business' from 'friendship,' but I am convinced that this blurring of the distinction is the foundation of community—and a fair explanation of why we do what we do.

Is this a big deal? Yes, it is everything.

# Working with Friends

Every once in a while, an acquaintance will share a *bon mote* of wisdom that they "don't do business with friends." Predictably, this insight will come shortly after letting me know that they have undertaken a project, but due to our "friendship," have hired another firm.

This business of doing business with friends, or more precisely, not doing business with friends, is an odd thing. Is the world of business so mercurial that one expects the natural course of business relationships to turn acrimonious and not be the predicate of great success? Maybe one should steer clear of the practice when hiring for an unsavory business, like performing a contract hit or mediating a divorce. But when an individual or a family commissions a custom home, expecting and accepting that the client-architect relationship will devolve and become adversarial is clearly counter to self-interest.

I've been fortunate enough to work with a great number of friends. I've lost one or two along the way, but probably not at a higher rate than other friendships which fade over time. More often than not, friendships have grown stronger by working together, and even more gratifyingly, we've made many new friends through project collaborations.

Residential architecture is founded on honesty, intimacy, personal exploration, and shared agendas: the same building blocks as friendship. I can't imagine anyone better to work with when designing a home than a friend, and in my experience, the deeper the friendship, the better the outcome. I have found this to be so universally true, that when someone claims to not want to work with friends, I reflexively question the quality and depth of their friendships.

Thinking about this has allowed us to identify a blind spot where we tend to treat everyone as friends and overextend ourselves, even when the chance of reciprocation may be slight. This culture became apparent when one of our dear friends and general contractors pulled me aside and earnestly stated that I needed to know the difference between a 'friend' and an 'acquaintance,' and that not everyone can be offered the same level of intimacy (or service). I am sure he is right, but if we have to sit on one side of this particular fence, I'll pick the side of making and working with friends every day. And to those acquaintances who would rather not, I wish them well, but hope for their sake that they have a change of heart. Perhaps they might benefit from one more screening of *It's a Wonderful Life*.

# Psychology 101

Psychology 101 in the spring semester of my freshman year was the most formative class in college. Although I only have a vague recollection of the professor's introduction to Freud, cognitive dissonance, and nature vs. nurture, the concepts stuck. Sitting in the back of the lecture hall as an eighteen-year-old—oftentimes dozing—it was impossible to forecast the impact the survey class would have upon my future studies and upon my career.

With apologies to many scores of studio professors, critics, and mentors, our penchant for sincere collaboration with clients grows from the syllabus of Psychology 101. Freud tells us that our impulses all stem from childhood experiences. I submit this observation is especially true of our architectural impulses, and my case is a particularly acute example. I wonder whether I would have chosen architecture as a course of study had it not been for my childhood home. Even many years later, I can still draw the home's floor plans with eyes closed, and I carry with me every day the deep emotions I felt and still feel for the house. Rotated forty-five degrees on its suburban lot, the modest house's passive solar design and flat roofs were strikingly unusual. East Grand Rapids, Michigan, was conservative in almost every regard, and a charcoal gray (black) flat-roofed house was far from ordinary. And yet, it turned out that our flat roof had little problem carrying snow loads, and leaks were no more common than those caused by ice dams at the pitched roofs of neighbors. My mother credited the house with inspiring her love of

Halloween. Her decorations, mostly flying witches, were left up year-round. I had mixed feelings. As a young teen, it was my chore to clean the yolk residue from airborne eggs hurled on devil's night. I suspect we would have been targeted less frequently if we lived in a Georgian colonial.

Were I reclining on a therapist's couch, I am certain the Freudian analyst would encourage me to look deeper than a favored holiday. My desire to fit in, to "join the club" and to be "normal" is, in large measure, a backlash from the social unease caused by having two scientists for parents, by both lighting the candles and putting up a tree, and by being small for my age (for any age). It never seemed to bother my parents that they were Jimmy Carter supporters in Jerry Ford's hometown, or that their retirement plan was to open an independent bookstore, and certainly not that we lived in a black house with a flat roof. The house was a visual testament to their desire to think and live differently. Together, my parents and my childhood home taught me many architectural lessons, and even more significantly, nurtured in me a willingness to take risks and to think for myself.

My design work is materially and specifically informed by my childhood, and many elements from that unusual house appear and reappear in our projects. The white brick fireplace and walls of books, the passive solar considerations, and the open kitchen in our current house where I cook in my mother's cast iron pans, are all derivative. Similarly, our clients come to us with strong aesthetic and functional preferences, many of which can be traced back to their childhoods. We are keen to learn these drivers, and just like analysts, we try to discover them in somewhat sneaky ways. Designing a home is an intimate process, and our clients need to be comfortable sharing their private wants and needs. We do not always get to the childhood roots, but we know they lurk under the surface. When we are fortunate to work on a multigenerational home—one for aggregated parents, children, grandparents, and grandchildren—the Freudian reality of childhood mixed with aging can be dramatic.

Another installment of Psychology 101, which I hazily yet vividly recall, presented the theory of cognitive dissonance. Many years after college and graduate school, and with decades of professional practice under my belt, I wrote an essay entitled "Some People Hate Walnut" about the theory of cognitive dissonance and its application in design. Paraphrasing the somewhat difficult to read Dr. Festinger (*A Theory of Cognitive Dissonance*, 1962), most people believe when choosing between two or more options that their selection is the objective best, provided the individual has made an affirmative selection after reasonable engagement – more so than after a coin flip or deference to a superficial or subjective preference. Although people second guess themselves, they are much less likely to do so after actively engaging in the decision-making process. If a child is given two pairs of shoes from which to choose, and if the child is afforded enough time to evaluate and come to an affirmative decision, it is very rare for the child to wish they had selected the other pair. The exact same process exists when adults participate in residential design decisions. The more time we spend working collaboratively with our clients, reviewing, debating, considering, reconsidering, and finally making decisions, the more certain we are that the decisions will be affirmed.

I like to think our Psychology 101 professor might have hoped we would connect Freud and Festinger. Many years later, I found the connection in a third concept from the class which brings them neatly together. Nature vs. nurture captivates my architectural thinking. In simplest terms, childhood is nature, and actively engaged adulthood is nurture. As I do with form vs. function, I quibble with the conjunction "vs." in nature vs. nurture. Just like form and function, these elements need not be oppositional to one another, but rather equally weighted for designs to be successful. Designing a home is deeply personal, and we seem to spend nearly as much time with our clients practicing a form of amateur therapy than we do discussing design specifics. Simplified, the role of the residential architect is to nurture our clients' nature. We bring together form and function, balance head and heart, and combine nature and nurture to ensure that every home we design meets and exceeds our clients' lofty expectations.

*Michael McKinley & Associates, LLC; Stonington, CT*

A famous sign outside an architect's office in Stonington, CT, proves that I am not the only architect who sat in the back of a survey class as a college freshman and put these thoughts together.

# Vocation : Avocation

For our Monday Morning Meetings, I have added an in-the-papers segment. I borrowed the concept wholesale from Pat Kiernan of NY1, whom I listen to most mornings and who reads the headlines that have grabbed his interest before arriving at the studio and going on air. One Monday, he included a headline from the *Wall Street Journal* that read, "Stop Telling Everyone What You Do for a Living; How to handle the "What do you do?" with aplomb and make more space for the rest of your life" (Rachel Feintzeig, 2023). The article's headline grabbed me like countless others about "quiet quitting," "the great resignation," and just about any article about working from home in athleisure or pajamas. These pandemic and post-pandemic subjects cause me to reflect on work-life balance: mine and that of our team.

For architects, the work-life balance oscillates between being on *charette*, a term coined at the Ecole des Beaux Artes - "being *en charette*," or literally drawing while sitting atop the cart as proctors rolled through the studio collecting presentation drawings - and hosting a boondoggle (never-ending happy hours). In the everyday language of employment, the polarized paradigm is expressed as a choice between exploitation and entitlement. Whether the phrase is industry specific or ubiquitous, an uncomfortable battle between work (pain) and leisure (pleasure) has taken root. From much of what we read in the papers and see on the news, at least in our progressive echo chamber, a shift toward the life side of the work-life balance is garnering the most attention.

During the second half of the 20th century, the iconic image of the modern architect was the fictional Howard Roark of Ayn Rand's *The Fountainhead* (1943), based on the very real Frank Lloyd Wright (1867-1959). Howard Roark's character was significantly drawn from the public exploits of Master Wright and their shared passion for perfection coupled with their larger-than-life personalities that left little room for balance. For Roark and Wright, there was no middle, just an unapologetic oscillation between extremes. While both stories make for breathless reading, there is not much to emulate if one is seeking equilibrium. If you ever wondered what the letter "A" in Type A stands for, perhaps it is for architect. Unfortunately, I believe the two figures were overly influential on the Architects of the late twentieth and 21st centuries, especially the "Starchitects." For employees, this meant endless hours for little or no pay and little or no opportunity for advancement, creating a hopelessness for those emerging from school and early in their careers.

When I emerged with my degree from graduate school, I was confronted with this lack of remuneration and a very certain career ceiling. I turned down a "starchitect" professor's internship offer - no pay and eighty hours per week—and formed a partnership with a graduate school classmate and my cousin, who was an established architect. We founded our firm based on principles of a good life-work balance, in direct response to a system not known for such. We chose not to work evenings or weekends, although I, for one, had little else to do. When we were fortunate enough to hire interns, they were paid. These "rules" and others—paid health care benefits, for instance—still exist today at the firm. This culture also informs our recent commitment to working remotely on Fridays, which began as a response to pandemic induced exhaustion and need for social distancing.

In these times of aspirational malaise, the field of architecture and others still tilt toward the intense side of the balancing scale. Becoming a doctor requires eight years of study, plus years in residency and the passing of one's boards. The law has its bar, long hours of practice, and billing requirements. Teachers collect their graduate degrees and go through near-constant continuing education and professional development. We professionals are proud of having met our education and apprenticeship requirements and take pleasure in indoctrinating (hazing) the younger generations. Thankfully, plenty of determined young people still sign up.

The recent pandemic and the media's push for a focus on leisure over labor will certainly take its toll on the professions as we waver slightly in our seemingly unidimensional pursuit of career success. But for those of us who declared our majors when we entered college, and who made it through graduate school and passed our exams, "quiet quitting" is the farthest thing from our minds. For us, the answer to the question of what we do is not awkward but rather an opportunity to celebrate our very identity. "I am a Doctor." "I am a Lawyer." "I am a Teacher." And in my case, "I am an Architect." I have always felt fortunate to have chosen a field that so many wistfully say they wanted to pursue but didn't for all manner of reasons. George Costanza's alter ego "Art Vandelay" on *Seinfeld* is our generation's testament to the sentiment. No matter the field or endeavor, I can only hope that the words of the poet Robert Frost resonate: "My goal in life is to unite my avocation with my vocation, as my two eyes made one in sight." (Two Tramps in Mud Time, 1936). Whomever we choose to be, may we all be so lucky as to have our avocations and our vocations be one.

*"Thirty Years Licensed and Insured." DFA Team t-shirt art for the 2023 New York Architects' Regatta Challenge*

# DESIGN MATTERS

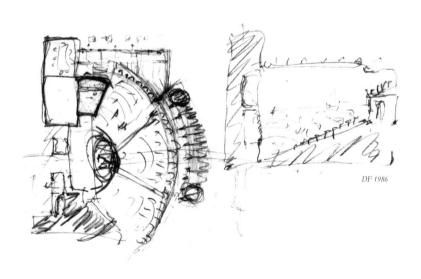

# Critical Romance

*"Critical Romance" featured on our business card.*

This writing comes easily. "Critical Romance" has been with me since the start and has been a guiding principal throughout my career. I began tinkering with the idea in graduate school and have written about it numerous times since. It's been a tag line on our business cards and part of our marketing materials since the mid 1990s.

I have always believed that architects and designers are driven into polarized camps. Either we believe in an engineer's methodology that all decisions relate to function, or we believe an academic or aesthetic priority should dictate design.

I believe in prioritizing neither and am certain that for design to succeed, the simultaneous satisfaction of both criteria is essential. Form can neither blindly follow function, nor can function solely follow form. Form and function are indivisible; the head and the heart are intertwined. "Critical Romance" is defined.

In balancing the head and the heart and by following our principles of "Critical Romance" (not to mention, "Yes, and…", and the K.I.S.S.

method), our best work has a timelessness and appears effortless. Our work balances form and function and is characterized by depth rather than surface or style.

# Nostalgia

Bored at home one day during the pandemic, I found myself leafing through a coffee table book, *100 Years of Iconic Toys* (2016), and was overcome by nostalgia, precisely as the editors intended. The book belongs to a genre of romantic documentary journalism that helps people connect through shared memories, in this case toys. The first chronologic entry in the book is "Marbles 1884" and the penultimate is "Kinetic Sand 2013." My children and I have played with both, as well as dozens of the featured toys from the years between. The last entry is "Frozen Dolls 2013," and for my children's generation, these dolls may someday elicit as much nostalgia as Lincoln Logs do for me. Studying the table of contents, I realize I probably relate to most of the material as much as or more than anyone. Thirty-two of the toys date from 1965, the year of my birth, to 1983, the year I graduated from high school. Many of the earlier offerings are still in production and a few of the more recent ones are favorites of my kids and are destined to create shared multigenerational memories. If you are curious, the full 129-year list of Roads Publishing's *100 Years of Iconic Toys* is in the Appendix of this book.

The Roads editorial team used a lot of curatorial judgment in compiling their toy history with each toy aspiring to be tagged as the Greatest of All Time (G.O.A.T.). I, for one, share their enthusiasm. Yet surprisingly, missing from the list is Monopoly (1935), Battleship (1967), the sports-oriented games like Matkot/Kadima (1932), and Trac Ball (1975). More notably, the curated collection skips over the technology games like Atari (1977), Nintendo (1983), and xBox (2001) - not to mention today's ubiquitous iPhone and iPad and every game their iPlatforms support. Whether you fondly remember playing on the floor with a Barrel of Monkeys, or expressing your creativity with an Etch A Sketch, or today play Candy Crush every time you take mass transit, or even that you still sleep with a teddy bear in spite of your age, the memory of toys of past eras and the addictiveness of today's digital offerings trigger very positive emotions. How can you not smile at the recollection of seeing a Slinky lurch and snake-walk down the stairs and at watching kids and grandchildren marvel just as you did? Other than a sad memory of a kinked spring (a Slinky is just an imaginatively branded coil spring) or the tragic loss of a childhood plaything, our memories of toys are almost without exception, romantically nostalgic.

I suspect each reader feels this nostalgia from simply reading words on the page, without any visuals. *100 Years of Iconic Toys* is a picture book, and while my descriptions are an affirmative testimonial, words cannot compete with the memories triggered by the book's photos. If only the book were also scratch-and-sniff, the sensory triggers would be complete. Close your eyes, and you can "see" your favorite toy, yet now imagine that toy is Play-Doh or Silly Putty. You can recall how it feels in your hand and even more vividly, how each toy's distinctive smell takes you back in time. Olfaction is widely understood to arouse the most intense memories, more than visuals and certainly more than words.

Adults enjoy strong memories of toys; toys usually played within the childhood home. For our clients, and for ourselves too, I think, recollections of childhood homes can equal and even exceed the nostalgia we feel for iconic toys. When working with homeowners for the first time, we often ask for pictures of their favorite homes. Sometimes, the images we receive are aspirational and other times less so, but as we dig deeper, we find that the strongest associations derive from childhood. Thank you, Dr. Freud. My childhood home was built in 1957 and was a flat-roofed, mid-century builder home, turned forty-five degrees on its suburban lot, and painted charcoal gray (black) with white trim and a red door. The builder must have been a follower of Charles and Ray Eames and their Case Study houses. As a young child, growing up in this split-level passive solar house, I had only a kid's understanding of its uniqueness, and I had no sense of how foundational the home would be to my career as an architect. I only knew the house was different from my friends' homes. To this day, I can easily draw floor plans from memory—and not solely because I am an architect. Many of the details I recall from this unusual and remarkable suburban house find their way into our work, often subconsciously. My childhood home had a white brick fireplace, as does ours today. My childhood home was sited to take advantage of the sun, as is ours today. Along similar lines, we have an attic fan to exhaust the hot summer air, just like we did when I was growing up. My childhood home had an open plan and the kitchen was the hub of the house, as is our kitchen today.

The suburban home in which I grew up was not a perfect house. The house was inexpensively constructed, required constant maintenance, and the acoustics were dreadful, unless of course, you enjoy hearing every word spoken in every other room. Had my parents been yellers, I doubt I could have recovered. Living in a black house attracted many airborne eggs on Halloween, and cleaning the residue from stained cedar siding was not easily accomplished. The basement wasn't a real basement, it was a concrete bunker and tornado shelter accessed by a ship's ladder. And yet, there was more good than bad - I like to think this is the case of every happy home, even one with a tornado shelter, crawlspace attic, and eggs on its face.

Two current-day stories remind me of the power of memories and nostalgia. The first is a story shared by a repeat client and friend whose insights I always value. After finishing renovation number one, we went out to dinner and spoke about the completed project and its impact on his day-to-day. He expressed that he and his wife regularly wake up noting how happy they are in their reimagined home, enjoying the functional successes and the beauty of the design elements, and that our work has meaningful daily impact on their lives. I've worked hard over the years to learn to accept a compliment, and while it doesn't come easily, I knew enough to say "thank you," and to try not to blush. The second part of the conversation was more unusual, and to me, more interesting. My friend shared that on certain mornings, he would step into his beautiful new master bathroom, only to somewhat inexplicably realize that he missed his old bathroom, no matter how dysfunctional and less beautiful when compared with the new. In spite of the objective differences, he experienced an unexpected and confusing nostalgia for the old space.

The second story is more personal. A few years ago, we built our dream home, and no matter how perfect—and it is pretty exceptional—our kids will once in a while remind me that they miss our old house – a 1400 square foot c. 1760 antique which often had a greater squirrel population than human. Nostalgia is extremely powerful, even when wholly detached from objective criteria.

With the above case studies in mind, it would seem that nostalgia would be high on our list of prescriptive design strategies. Simply find out what a client remembers most fondly about a childhood home and replicate those elements. While such an approach may be to some degree fruitful, a more thorough study is in order before blithely adopting nostalgia as a design tool. Until the 20th century, romantic nostalgia was the basis of most architectural expression. From the Renaissance and Greek Revival to the Beaux Arts, nostalgia for a former era or epoch was universal. The Industrial Revolution, Art Nouveau, and even Frank Lloyd Wright's Prairie Style all incorporated details from previous eras. Not until the Bauhaus school and the International Style, did architects and designers disengage from historic precedent. With the predictability of a pendulum, the 1980s and 1990s brought a resurgence of historic referentialism in in the form of the Post-Modern movement. Thirty years later, we are enjoying a mid-century modern revival, based upon an extremely stylish and popular yet equally referential design language. When I was an undergraduate, we looked upon Jefferson's Monticello and the Academical Village at the University of Virginia as primary sources, establishing the foundational underpinning of our studies. At the same time, we were taught that Palladio's la Rotonda was the inspiration for Jefferson's two masterpieces - even the revolutionary and innovative Jefferson borrowed sources.

As a graduate student at Columbia University in New York City, with the deconstructionist architect Bernard Tschumi as dean, we were taught that all historic precedent should be cast aside and that a reverential or nostalgic approach to design was unfounded, and anything but innovative—even though Deconstructionism borrowed heavily from early 20th century Constructivism. By the time I set out on my own, there was zero consensus in the Academy as to whether nostalgia was a romantic or pejorative concept, and today, perhaps more than ever, the battle lines are starkly drawn. On one side are the Classicists, promoting designs borrowed from and exalting a former era, and on the other are the Post-Deconstructionists designing iconoclastic buildings of warped planes and acute angles, and willing to tear down architectural monuments with little concern for heritage. Armed with an appreciation of both schools of thought, I suggest a more centrist philosophy. Form need not follow function, nor function follow form—both can reinforce each other. Nostalgia and innovation can and need to coexist, celebrating the best of what has come before, while steadfastly embracing and imagining all that has yet to be.

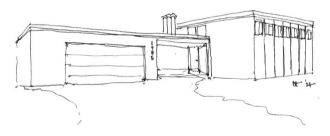

*My Childhood Home, 1505 Pinecrest Ave SE, East Grand Rapids, MI*

# Modern Preservation

During the summer of 1986, I traveled and studied in Vicenza, Italy with fellow UVA architecture students. We were for the most part impressionable undergraduates and our professors enjoyed introducing us in person and in situ to the majestic works of Renaissance maestro Andrea Palladio and, at the other end of the spectrum, to those of the modernist virtuoso Carlo Scarpa. Reconciling the two was the singular genius of our teacher, and founder of the first study abroad programs at UVA, Mario di Valmarana. To paraphrase Mario, whom I came to know well over subsequent decades, "The architect has a great responsibility to steadfastly and aggressively preserve that which is deserving, but when conservation is not warranted, to design and build in a manner that enhances that which came before." What was so spectacular and liberating about Mario's teachings was that he found Palladio and Scarpa not oppositional, but rather, equally worthy of adulation and celebration.

Design is very personal, and it has taken me years to find my voice, much of which reaches back to lessons taught by Mario (and many others). For me, combining modern intervention with historic appreciation is as foundational as balancing form and function. A second lesson we learnt from Mario is that historic structures need to be utilized, not turned into museums. We cry when landmarks are destroyed, yet we cannot thrive and prosper in museums, no matter how much we enjoy visiting them.

After years of reflection, I believe that Mario's teaching can be synthesized as a quest for rigorous sincerity. If we follow his lead, we will succeed at satisfying today's challenges through exuberant design, while simultaneously endeavoring to preserve our history and architectural heritage for future generations.

Note: Sadly, we lost Mario in 2010, and his family asked that I speak at his memorial service. I wrote my remarks the night before, and as short as they were, I barely made it through. A few months later, one of my friends shared that I am indeed a terrible public speaker. I only hope that my comments were better than my delivery, or my handwriting. If you can follow along, my remarks are copied here:

*Sketch by Mario di Valmarana*

BARBOURSVILLE, VIRGINIA    11·20·2010

FARMINGTON COUNTRY CLUB

IT IS NICE TO BE BACK IN BARBOURSVILLE, A PLACE THAT BRINGS
BACK SO MANY FINE MEMORIES OF FALL DAYS SPENT WITH
WATERCOLORS AND WINE. TODAY, I AM HERE WITH YOU, FRIENDS
AND FAMILY, STUDENTS AND COLLEAGUES TO REMEMBER MARIO.
MANY OF YOU KNEW MARIO BETTER, AND FOR LONGER, AND YET I
FEEL I CAN SPEAK FOR EVERYONE GATHERED HERE; THAT WHILE
WE EACH WILL MISS HIM, WE ARE INFINITELY BETTER FOR HAVING
KNOWN HIM. MARIO BROUGHT TO ALL HIS ACTIVITIES AND RELATIONSHIPS
A PASSION AND A PROFOUND SENSE OF HUMANITY. IT IS NO WONDER
SO MANY OF US HAVE COME TODAY.
—
WHILE MARIO TAUGHT ARCHITECTURE, AND TAUGHT IT WELL, HIS
TEACHING WENT WELL BEYOND HIS TREASURED SLIDES AND TIRELESS
WALKING TOURS. FOR ME, HE CONVEYED, IN A POWERFUL
AND POSITIVE WAY, WHAT IT MEANS, AND SHOULD MEAN, TO BE
AN ARCHITECT. HE SOUGHT, I BELIEVE, TO TEACH THE ESSENCE
OF ARCHITECTURE — TO FIGHT TO PRESERVE THAT WHICH IS
IMPORTANT AND VALUABLE AND BEAUTIFUL, AND YET TO GO
FORWARD WITH RELEVANCE WHEN CREATING ANEW.

HE SHARED WITH ALL HIS UNFLAGGING OPTIMISM, HIS HUMOR,
AND HIS LEADERSHIP. HIS EXAMPLE IS ONE FOR US TO
REMEMBER AND TO FOLLOW, AND AS WE DO, I KNOW HE
WOULD BE SMILING.

I AM FORTUNATE AND HONORED TO HAVE KNOWN MARIO, T HAVE
BEEN TAUGHT BY HIM, AND MOST OF ALL TO HAVE CALLED
HIM MY FRIEND.

DANIEL FRISCH
VICENZA, 1986
BS ARCHITECTURE, 1987

1625 COUNTRY CLUB CIRCLE    CHARLOTTESVILLE, VA 22901-5030    www.farmingtoncc.com
TEL 434 296-5661    FAX 434 977-5924

# Wite-Out

Where would we be without "Wite-Out"?

From Wikipedia:

*Wite-Out dates to 1966, when Edwin Johanknecht an insurance-company clerk, sought to address a problem he observed in correction fluid available at the time: a tendency to smudge ink on photostatic copies when it was applied. Johanknecht enlisted the help of his associate George Kloosterhouse, a basement waterproofer who experimented with chemicals, and together they developed their own correction fluid, introduced as "Wite-Out WO-1 Erasing Liquid".*

*In 1971, they incorporated as Wite-Out Products, Inc. The trademark "Wite-Out" was registered by the United States Patent and Trademark Office on February 5, 1974. (The application listed the date of "first use in commerce" as January 27, 1966.)*

*Early forms of Wite-Out sold through 1981 were water-based and hence water-soluble. While this allowed simple cleaning, it also had the problem of long drying times. The formula also did not work well on non-photostatic media such as typewritten copy.*

*The company was bought in 1981 by Archibald Douglas. Douglas, as chairman, led the company toward solvent-based formulas with faster drying times. Three different formulas were created, each optimized for different media. New problems arose: a separate bottle of thinner was required, and the solvent used was known to contribute to ozone depletion. The company addressed these problems in July 1990 with the introduction of a reformulated "For Everything" correction fluid.*

*In June 1992, Wite-Out Products was bought by the BIC Corporation. BIC released a number of new products under its newly acquired brand, including a Wite-Out ballpoint pen (November 1996) and dry correction tape (1998).*

At the firm, "Wite-Out" has survived, outlasting the T-Square, the Mayline, the typewriter, the fax machine, the pocket diary, the Rolodex, the Fil-o-Fax, the beeper, the Palm Pilot, the Blackberry, and a baker's dozen of Steve Jobs' i-Launches. Around 1992, soon after hanging our shingle and about the same time Bic bought Wite-Out, we were given a Mac SE, replacing our trusty typewriter for proposals and correspondence. We were hooked and became Apple acolytes, unaware that this gift of a single first-generation Mac would contribute so much to our culture and identity. Computers quickly became essential to our communication and to our work product, most notably in 1997 when we switched from hand drafting to CAD (Computer-Aided Design). The transition was challenging; software was early in its development and prone to bugs, hardware and software were expensive, and platforms communicated poorly with one another. Unfortunately, this was especially true for those of us steadfastly committed to the Apple community and the gestalt.

Even though I was still young and loved being "on the boards," I skipped the CAD tutorials. I was convinced, as I remain today, that drafting alongside our production team would be a misallocation of my time. Many graduates who come and interview with DFA are intrigued by my complete lack of CAD fluency, not fully understanding that being CAD-illiterate allows me to focus on my leadership roles, while simultaneously affording our associates more autonomy and responsibility.

As the firm evolved and became ever more reliant on technology, we stayed loyal to Apple, not switching to the Windows-based AutoCad platform, even though software for the Mac lagged terribly. For years, we had trouble sharing files with engineers, and even our professional association, the American Institute of Architects (AIA), failed to offer contract templates formatted for the Mac. In response, we purchased a lone PC machine to access these forms and to run other Windows-exclusive software. Only in the last few years has the interaction between platforms become (almost) seamless, validating our decision to stay with Apple through all the troughs and valleys.

I remember with ambivalent fondness the following catalog: our initial Mac SE, the Mac Classic II, the Mac Quadra, the original iMac in "Bondi Blue" (the paint color we chose for our powder room in 1997), the Power Mac G3, G4, and G5 (they were insanely heavy when brought to TekServe to repair), the Mac Mini, the Mac Pro, and now, finally, our 27" iMac's, which I know will invariably become obsolete as well, even if I can't see how.

We all now have iPhones and iPads, and many of us have laptops; I purchased my first MacBook to write these essays. A shelf in Jamie's office has become a technology museum of older Apple computers and in my office, I have a mid-century bar cart displaying a collection of digital point-and-shoots, flip phones, Blackberries, and early-generation iPhones. The younger associates in our office, who use technology with great facility are too young to have nostalgia for an earlier generation's electronica, probably find our collections odd, and are bemused by my low-tech methods and especially by my reliance on and reverence for "Wite-Out".

Every week, we receive inquiries about potential projects, frequently concerning potential apartment renovations or combinations of multiple apartments. Whenever tasked with evaluating such a project, I print a copy of the floor plan and take out "Wite-Out" and study the possibilities. Although it takes a long time for a project to go from the idea stage to move-in, many of our completed projects are the direct product of these preliminary "Wite-Out" assessments.

"Wite-Out" remains an indispensable tool in our creative process. It's not easy to use. Due to its water content, it dries slowly and pen strokes bleed on top of it, meaning everything smears. Embarrassingly, I often find myself at dinner with a mixture of ink and "Wite-Out" covering my hands. For me, though, this very low-tech process is how I respond to the challenge of designing a home. While patiently waiting for a composition to dry, my mind sees the problem before me more clearly, and fixing a smudged drawing usually results in meaningful refinement.

I believe and teach that hand-drawing and model-making remain primary and foundational tools and are still essential, even considering the technologic capability and advancements brought by CAD and 3-D printing. Clarity of thought is frequently obscured by the intellectual distance between the designer and the CAD drawing being produced. In the same vein, I have rarely met someone who successfully synchronizes original thought with keystrokes. While it takes training and proficiency to draw using a computer, the emphasis often shifts from creative exploration to document production. With pen and paper and X-Acto knives, our thoughts flow more freely.

I (obsessively) dwell on technology, and not just as it relates to architectural design. I am known to be a resistant and plodding adopter, even while I wholly endorse the indisputable benefits of our digital age and recognize that our future will be infinitely brighter with universal access to technology. Like most parents, I worry about an overreliance on technology, and about screen time and social media. How much is too much, both for our youngest generation and for ourselves?

One of my favorite responsibilities at the office and at home is to demonstrate that the human touch - including my smeared hand drawings - is more compelling than machine alternatives. To accomplish this, I seek to inspire a love of non-technology-based endeavors, rather than to advocate for technology deprivation. Not only would an attempt to deprive fail in the face of the very seductive technology products, it would also be quite hypocritical. We promote our business on Instagram, Alexa shuffles our music at home and keeps the timer on the kids' baking, our 3-D renderings explain and inspire, and the Spelling Bee offering of my *NY Times* digital subscription is my go-to escape on the subway (replacing my short-lived Candy Crush addiction). We are plugged-in 24/7 and our dependence on and enthusiasm for technology will only grow over time.

Notwithstanding, nothing compares to happy hour, team sports, Main Street and shopping local, band practice, dinner table conversation and heated arguments, hand drawing, model making, board games, and reading hardcover books. We'll continue to embrace email, Wikipedia, social media, and CAD, taking every advantage of each new technology, but along the way, here's hoping Papermate continues to make Flair pens, and that Bic continues to make "Wite-Out." We're loyal customers.

# Programming

Monday morning brings me great pleasure, and I always look forward to presenting broad and foundational themes.

Sharing and discussing ideas on Monday mornings, we collectively identify the building blocks that define our work. Successful projects are formed early, combining a nuanced understanding of project program coupled with creative and insightful schematic designs. Creating a robust project program demands a deep dive, assessing, challenging, and refining the initial criteria of a client's wish list. Helping a client understand and define their program is, perhaps, the most significant role a residential architect performs.

The first phase of professional services enumerated within our standard form of agreement is "programming." At a basic level, a program documents the project requirements, including the obvious functional priorities such as the number of bedrooms, or the importance of a view, and the project budget. A more nuanced program also includes a stylistic set of priorities, even if these priorities are less clear than the functional or economic necessities. Every project has a wish list, and most clients come to the first meeting with their architect with a good idea of their priorities. While a client may come prepared with a preconceived understanding of needs and desires, it is our task to help further define, refine, and elaborate a more robust program including subjective goals far beyond the pragmatic. The process is at once analytic and intimate. Why is a project being considered, and what does it mean to the client? Do the economic priorities consider investment stewardship or availability of capital? Are we being commissioned to build a home that might be sold in a few years, or is the hope that the home sustains future generations? Do spouses agree on these issues and countless others? The programming phase can simultaneously bring clarity and create confusion.

Social-emotional issues further complicate issues. Is it a project priority to showcase the client's success, or perhaps, to conceal? Is the home to be designed to entertain with the expectation of a continual house party? Will they host dinner parties worthy of a dedicated formal dining room? If the living room does not have a TV will it be used? And finally, aesthetic considerations need to be reviewed, as early as in the pre-design programming phase. Will the project be traditional or modern, historicist or futurist?

Schematic design, which follows programming, is filled with optimism and creativity and is the most exciting phase of any project. While flawless execution during each phase of the design and construction process is essential, schematics set the table. It has taken us years of study and practice to realize that a rewarding schematic design phase is not the kick-off, but the product of first-rate programming.

# A, B, & C

If I were to spend time lounging on a psychiatrist's Eames Chair, my analyst might conclude that the kids and I have binge-read too much Roald Dahl and Dr. Seuss, and certainly, that I have been an architect for far too many years. Many nights in the deepest of sleep, I wander through a home entirely of my own imagination, invariably vacant and in spectacular disrepair. As I explore, I discover secret passages leading to ever larger, more fantastic, and more desperate spaces. Eventually in these dreams, I begin imagining the Sisyphean tasks of restoration and renovation. Even in my dreams, there just isn't enough capital for either the purchase or for renovations and I wake up sweating.

Whether building a ground-up home or renovating a studio apartment, most projects are aspirational and resource intensive, both in time and money. When beginning the schematic design process, I often invent an imaginary rich uncle, one who has been kind enough to bequeath to me a property as well as the funds with which to build. How would I prioritize needs and wants if I had a fixed amount of money and no access to more? Even in a dream state, failing to recognize the paramount nature of budgetary constraints would be like staring at the teeth of my imaginary gift horse.

I believe my dreams also stem from having lived and practiced in New York City for so many years. New York City is a mirage. A majority of people come from elsewhere, work hard, and (mostly) succeed. At some point, they announce their success by setting out to purchase an apartment, penthouse, or townhouse. Unlike my dreams, I've rarely toured a home with a potential buyer that was not one room too small or too inexpensive. To make matters worse, construction costs and logistic challenges are certain to threaten fiscal controls. To maintain budget as a priority, homeowners will sometimes share a story of limited resources and will elevate financial considerations above all.

In helping a client budget for construction, whether for a new house or a modest apartment renovation, we work to establish an equilibrium between wants and needs, and to balance head and heart. Setting a budget for a new home is fairly straightforward: determine the size and the general quality and then compare with completed projects. Establishing a budget for a renovation is a little less so. While introductory conversations are usually based upon a client's clear and predetermined vison, most initial thoughts and expectations about scope and budget are dramatically underestimated. To adapt a phrase, "if I had a dollar for every gut renovation that has been presented as a cosmetic project, I'd be a wealthy architect." When evaluating the balance between discretionary and necessary, we utilize a simplistic and disarming algorithm we call "A, B, or C."

An "A" project type is one in which the scope can be contained and is unlikely to expand. This may be a stand-alone kitchen or bath renovation whose scope will not extend to installing central air, room reconfigurations, and a complete rewiring and repainting of the entire residence. We refer to these "A" projects contained within zippered enclosures as surgical interventions.

A "B" project is described by having many acceptable or even well-liked components, but where the intended scope touches many areas. These "B" projects represent the majority of projects to which we are introduced. Usually, the buyer repeatedly asserts and assures that the project is "not a gut," and that the intended scope is minimal—really a cosmetic project. Ninety perccent of the time, these "B" projects evolve to become full-scope undertakings. Real estate agents predictably reinforce scope underestimation by presenting favorable marketing materials. Properties, even ones in estate condition, are shown in their best light and are easier to sell if represented this way. Purchasers become willing partners in this deception, usually confident of the acceptability of certain shortcomings of a particular property or believing work could be performed down the road. While realtors have the experience to dig deeper, they lack incentive, and buyers who don't have the means, time, or desire to fully renovate complicitly cooperate.

Earlier in our careers, we were more willing to accommodate partial scope expectations, even when we were skeptical. When consulting with homeowners, we learned to rigorously assess scope and establish realistic project budgets. First, we start with what is behind the walls, not just the cosmetic details. Would it make sense, for instance, to skim coat and paint an entire apartment without checking the wiring in the walls? We have also found many renovated apartments with floors that were not replaced when previous renovations were performed, and it is very difficult to replace a floor after the fact. Similarly, most buildings in Manhattan do not allow for the replacement of bathroom fixtures and retiling without replacing the branch piping behind the walls and replacing the shower valves with code compliant anti-scald valves and water hammer arrestors. As a project's scope increases to include wiring and plumbing work, costs increase, and not electively so. Categories like air-conditioning and window replacements tip the scales. Installing proper air conditioning with all of the associated costs still presents a meaningful return on investment, both from a lifestyle and monetary viewpoint. We have found our clients have enjoyed the greater appreciation in value after performing full renovations when compared to partial or cosmetic renovations. Few new buyers want to pay for a previous homeowner's personal decoration, but almost all buyers are interested in buying a home that has had its electric upgraded, its bathrooms renovated, its kitchen redone, and has central air and new windows—provided the work is technically and aesthetically well executed.

In addition to evaluating the systemic needs of a project, we also review the discretionary choices, many of which also tip the scales towards scope creep and wholesale renovations. An example I frequently quote is "doors and hardware." Predictably, several new door openings are necessitated by layout changes, and several doors are scheduled to remain. Should the new doors, hardware, and trim be fabricated and installed to match the existing, or will the owner prefer to replace all the doors, hardware, and trim to a new (improved) standard? It's very hard to endorse making new installations match substandard existing conditions. Even the best items of a previous renovation usually look dated or tired when placed next to new work.

In the end, our clients learned their original – and certain – plan of a "B" project might be ill considered, and that they would be wise to either limit the scope of the project and proceed with an "A" project or embrace scope-creep. To finish the alphabetical allegory, a "C" project is, therefore, a fully considered project for which the entire client program has been evaluated. After going through the three project types, our renovation projects invariably default to the "A" and "C" categories.

Using our "A, B, or C" algorithm also provides a framework when touring out-of-city projects and assessing potential scope. If I were given a second dollar for every time I've been told a house was definitely not a tear-down... Just as in the city, a more surgical intervention is sometimes the best option. Whether in the city or in the country, we are keen to go through this scope analysis, budget, and value assessment when buyers are considering an acquisition, rather than after they have signed contracts. It is much easier to adjust budget and schedule expectations and to set projects on solid footings before attending the closing.

# So... It's Not a Tear-Down?

Once upon a time, before the great recession and well before the COVID-19 pandemic, most of our projects were in Manhattan. Our days were spent preparing plans for apartment renovations and combinations and for townhouses and penthouses. Based on data compiled from completed projects, I speak and write of the formulaic A, B, C's of renovations. We developed this letter-based classification system to help set client expectations and place projects on solid footing from acquisition to completion. "A" projects were surgical interventions, perhaps a stand-alone kitchen or bath renovation, or maybe limited to painting the walls or refinishing floors. These small projects were easily contained and executed. "B" projects were brought to us frequently by clients who proposed significant renovations yet were happy with many aspects of a property. Invariably, these projects turned into wholesale renovations, or "C" projects. We often tell stories of clients who insisted they wanted to save and refinish the floors, even though they were asking for new central air conditioning, rewiring the apartment, and installing a new kitchen and bathrooms, not to mention replacing the windows. After all this assessment, it usually becomes clear to the homeowner that, from an investment standpoint, it would be irresponsible not to replace the floors. Knowing our A, B, Cs in NYC help us properly advise buyers pre-acquisition and preserves friendships by helping to avoid projects that were much larger in scope than initially projected.

For many years, New York City was our primary laboratory, and with decades of data at our disposal, we became quite capable at predicting budgets and timelines for projects. Starting with the Great Recession and accelerated by the COVID-19 Pandemic, we find many of our new projects have migrated out of the city—whether home renovations, additions, or ground-up homes. As our focus shifted from city to country, we started to study project dynamics to see if we could find similarities to the A, B, and C's of our city projects. Several recent projects help us answer the question of whether to renovate or demolish and start anew, a question very much akin to those we had asked in the city. Our first example is a summer cottage dating from the early 20th century, which had been only marginally updated through the years. At our first meeting, the client told me that she had met with a design-build competitor who works frequently in our community and who dismissively insisted that the cottage was without question a tear-down. I knew the other designer's work and thought the assessment to be reflexive and quite possibly self-interested, and I sold hard the idea that my firm would diligently study a renovation alternative, although in the end, we came to the same conclusion. Once the owner's expectations and program were understood, and plans prepared, we realized that the cottage had outlived its usefulness, needed to be torn down, and now, a beautiful new home stands in its stead.

As the COVID-19 pandemic waned, we began working with a client who owned a similarly modest cottage on the opposite shore of the same lake. They were empty-nesting weekenders who loved their cozy 1200 square foot cottage, but knew it was time to update it, and if possible, to enlarge it. Having been referred to us by a neighbor, for whom we had designed a much larger house that may well have filled the cottage's entire site if moved a half mile down the road, our new patrons were nervous about over-enlarging. Their aspirations were modest, but the cottage would certainly benefit from being modernized and expanded a bit. With much of the cottage residing within the postage-stamp sized lot's rear yard setback, we proposed a minimal as-of-right enlargement at the front of the house and a stand-alone screened porch to the side, and of course, a fantastic hot tub in which to soak and from which to soak in the view. The project was one of our smaller non-urban projects, so we spent exponentially more time on a relative basis developing our plans and details, and then we sent it to three of our favorite contractors to bid. One declined and the other two came back with estimates well outside of the project's budget parameters. While the clients had the wherewithal to approve an increased project budget, enthusiasm waned, and the plans were set aside.

Our post-mortem debriefings with the bidders revealed that the decision to consider the project as an extensive renovation with minimal additions was penny-wise and had negatively impacted the project's value proposition. We had proposed excavating the home's basement, reconfiguring the first and second floors, modifying the roof lines, re-wring, replacing the mechanical systems, and refreshing the home's finishes and materials. What we heard—and what we have heard many times—is that the extensive surgery of working around an existing structure adds exponential cost when compared with straight replacement. With the memory of the previous plans, we started over. We premised the new approach on the demolition of the cottage and a resiting of the home forward on the lot, where we would not be limited to the original non-conforming footprint set largely within the rear yard setback. While the new design was only ten percent larger than that originally proposed, the new design featured more modern ceiling heights and the screen porch is now attached rather than being a glorified gazebo. While more expensive in actual dollars, the new house will be, without question, a better value proposition than the original, and even more importantly will be a better product by any metric.

If our experience were limited to these first two examples, we could easily draw the conclusion that we had found a house renovation credo akin to our New York City A, B, & C's. Careful assessment at the onset of a project would result in tearing down rather than renovating. A study of additional examples, however, muddies the waters.

A next example demonstrates a slightly modified answer to the question of whether a project is a renovation or a tear-down. On a lake twenty miles to the south of the previous two case studies, we were working with homeowners who were reasonably happy with their lakeside weekend home, even though they had a long wish list of deferred maintenance and significant landscape work due to years of run-off-based erosion.

When we started the programming process with the owners, the focus was on the immediate needs, landscaping, and replacing a deck that had rotted and was in danger of collapse. As we dug further, we learned that the grievances with the circa 2000 house were greater than first represented. The kitchen and baths were outdated, the relationship between inside and outside was meager, and the HVAC systems dated to a previous generation and warranted wholesale replacement. And just like a city project, the list kept growing, including the want of better thermal and sound insulation throughout the house. Our assessment, as it had been with so many others, was that the home's systems had outlived their lifespan, and the house would benefit from extensive surgery and a wholesale reimagination. That is, until we received bids for the home we designed. It turns out we hadn't learned as much as we thought from our New York experience, or from examples one and two. The surgery we proposed was simply too great to be a reasonable value proposition. So back to the CAD drawing board we went, with the premise that a near-total tear down might make sense. Like the first example, we again started over, and proposed that the existing house be demolished; but that the existing foundation, swimming pool, and septic system remain. During the redesign phase, we also reduced the square footage and simplified the structural interventions. All told, the redesigned house better satisfied the homeowners' program and simultaneously reduced construction costs by approximately twenty-five percent. In this example, we learned that the answer to renovate or tear down is to mostly demolish an existing home, but also, to make good use out of the home's siting and foundation.

My most personal example is our own house. On December 12, 2012, we purchased on a fifty-six acre farm a mile from my wife's childhood home. The "farm" was mostly a forested billy-goat hill and marshland in Kent Hollow, CT, whose only structure was a 19th century tobacco barn with sprung boards and a leaky roof. A small herd of Herefords slept in the dirt at the lower level of the bank barn, while holes in the floor above acted as their skylights. The heart of the property was a three-acre donut hole at its center with a dilapidated house and a garage on a small parcel across the road that did not convey with the farm. We surmise the farming family who had last acquired the farm in 1917 must not have needed the farmhouse, or the previous owner wanted to remain after the sale of their lands. The house and garage were in foreclosure and had fallen on hard times. Our bid won at the foreclosure auction, and we closed on the purchase on my wife's birthday. When I shared with her that we had closed on such an auspicious day, she humorously quipped, "oh, you bought me a tear-down for my birthday." We learned a great deal through the foreclosure process, including that there were IRS liens on the property and that the IRS had a six-month right to purchase the house at our strike price if the agency wanted to try to recoup any excess equity. Once the tolling period was over, we took stock. Should we build across the river on the hillside, should we tear down the house—it seemed likely to collapse on its own—and rebuild a little further from the road, or just demolish the house and hold the land for future development? With the squatters having moved on, selective demolition uncovered an original hand-hewn circa 1760 timber frame which had been hidden beneath sagging 20th century additions.

We demolished everything but the frame and roof sheathing complete with thousands of cut nails. The frame was shored and stabilized, a new foundation poured beneath, and the two large brick chimneys were largely rebuilt. We then built a new home in and around this period frame. While a tear-down would have been both more efficient and less expensive, we would not be able to humorously debate our neighbors about who lives in the oldest house in the Hollow. And while a new home would have been located far greater than eleven feet from the road, our new home stands as if it has always been there, as in fact, it has since before the Revolutionary War. As both an architect and a homeowner, there is no greater satisfaction than preserving and living in a structure with such significant history.

After a full assessment of these four projects and many others, we have come to see similarities and differences between our formulaic A, B, & C's of apartment renovations and the more nuanced considerations of whether to renovate or demolish a single family home looking to its next chapter. The variables in the country defer to a careful assessment of the historic or economic value in the structure. Taking the case studies in order, the first two homes were not worth saving and more significantly, each stood in the way of accomplishing the homeowner's programmatic goals. The third example was similar, except the foundation and site improvements represented retained value, delivering logistic, environmental, and economic benefits to the homeowners. In the last, our saving of an original frame on an original site seemed modest at first but only grew in significance.

Collectively, our studies, practice, and teachings lead me to believe that if something is worth preserving, you fight to do so regardless of the economic consequences or inconvenience. While we often validate the need for wholesale replacement of structures that are too difficult to save, we are proud of trying absolutely everything before we call in the wrecking crew.

# Slowly, Over Time

When meeting people for the first time or when interviewing for a project, question number one is likely to be, "So, what is your style?" Early in my career, I struggled with the question. Now, having designed our house, our apartment, and our office, I predictably answer by giving a tour, in-person or virtually. The two homes and the office have different architectural DNA, but share a cluttered yet curated eclectic identity.

We've completed projects in various paradigms, from rigorous preservation and restoration projects to modern ground-up homes. My personal history and references are similarly diverse. I grew up amidst conformity in western Michigan in a non-conformist, flat-roofed, charcoal gray, passive-solar house set askew on its suburban lot. In college, we studied Jefferson's works in Charlottesville and Palladio's villas in the Veneto. To confuse matters further, deconstructivism was the design currency du jour during my graduate studies at Columbia University. Choosing a singular style never occurred to me.

When it comes to design in practice, we seek to find a language that supports and satisfies the unique sensibilities of the individual homeowner. This is the heart of enlightened client service, an engagement that resists egoistic self-expression and a one-style-fits-all design vision. As practitioners, we have become fluent in varied design languages, and our projects, both in scale and style, reflect this. Great design that transcends stylistic categorization is the product of rigorous study, organic development, and the balancing of form and function.

I was reminded recently—in a most personal way—that all design strategies are not equal and that traditional design, which is often dismissively thought to be easy, is as difficult or even more so than designing in the modern vernacular. My wife Darcy and I drove down from our home in Kent, CT, to Redding, CT, for a celebration of life event for a friend's mother, Marisa Bisi Erskine, who had passed away soon after her 100th birthday. Her daughter Silvia is a practicing architect and landscape architect with degrees in both from the University Virginia. Silvia and I graduated in different years, but we both studied in Vicenza and participate as alumni practitioners in UVA's study abroad programs in the Veneto, and we also collaborate on projects here at home. The party was held at the house that Silvia, Silvia's partner Tom, a retired airline pilot and novelist, Silvia's mom, and Phoebe, the family dog, all shared, and the event was nothing short of spectacular. Family and friends all realized that they had gathered for a celebration of a really, really, good life. And while each reminiscence was more touching and memorable than the one before, I found the home itself to be an equally powerful testament.

The oldest portion of the house dates to the 18th century, with the most recent additions having been built after the mother and daughter purchased the property in 2004. Silvia integrated the design of the additions and gardens to blend seamlessly with the much older structure. I once heard this strategy described by a Litchfield County resident responding to one of our projects as "New England Additive Architecture."

The seamlessness reminds me of a wager I have with the associates in my office, that when we are looking for inspiration for renovations and additions to an older home, I am happy to buy lunch should an associate return with a photograph of a successful addition and not one where a modern structure is appended to an older structure (like I.M. Pei's pyramid in the courtyard of the Louvre). While exuberant modern additions to historic homes can be exciting and satisfying to both architects and homeowners, it is harder to find examples of integrated additions than one might think.

As impressive as the coherence and elegance of the architecture of the Redding house is, the furnishings and decoration do a much better job of telling the story of the inhabitants. The decorations, art, and books tell of a personal style, and with a genuineness that cannot be fabricated. When decorating with a modern palette, everything can be coordinated and precisely styled. And yet, we all recall the cringeworthy stories of Edgar Kauffmann bringing Frank Lloyd Wright's furniture back to the house when Wright would visit. While Fallingwater is a masterwork and one of the finest examples of 20th century American residential architecture, Master Wright supplanted Mr. Kaufmann as the primary actor.

When walking through Marisa, Silvia, Tom, and Phoebe's home, as we did that day, a corner cannot be turned without being reminded of the gaiety of the inhabitants. Separate living rooms, or more accurately drawing rooms, flank a central kitchen and dining room where the generations can cook and dine together. The public rooms all look out on the formal gardens and the distant views. Books, art, and music abound. And the sitting areas, which are too numerous to count, beckon the family and guests to sit quietly in conversation or to lose oneself in the shared and solitary passion for literature.

The house in Redding is exactly the home many designers aspire to simulate and rarely achieve. Designers can fill a home with antiques, period pieces, and walls of books, but a well-lived life cannot be sourced by purchasing someone else's collections. Traditional design requires sincerity and the passionate and engaged participation of its patron. In almost every room, the most recent book lies ready to be picked up, just where the reader had last put it down, and the favorite blanket lays on a small settee in case Phoebe might chose to come out of hiding to nap in a preferred library nook. I imagine the sprays of flowers do not appear every day, but one notes the miniature citrus trees on the terrace, so lovingly tended and potted, rather than planted for when they are brought into the house during the winter.

The decorations and lifestyle are not commoditized, contrived, or aspirational. Rather, the home is an honest embodiment and representation of the homeowners' shared personalities. Quirky in places, cluttered at times, and always in need of touch-ups, the house is an extension of body and soul. Even filled with people, the house asserts a sense of privacy and intimacy, its spaces to be shared with family and loved ones, slowly over time.

Coming full circle, I return to my own homes (and office) and the question of my own style, hoping to give a more nuanced answer than simply, "come visit." While I admire and am awed by so many architect-designed homes where the architecture is the art – from La Rotonda to Monticello to Chareau's Maison de Verre (Glass House), to Phillip Johnson's own Glass House, to Fallingwater, I prefer a quieter architecture that does not aspire, dominate, or compete.

I feel our two homes and the office each have an old soul, wholly different than Silvia and Tom's but similar in substance. We enjoy art that was collected by our parents or made by artist-friends. We use my mother's cast iron pans every day. Unless we have recently prepared for a party or a photo shoot, there is always a frustrating amount to do – everything from shelving books that have accumulated on every surface to weeding the gardens and catching up with ongoing maintenance projects. A home should not, and really cannot be something fixed in time, but an ever-evolving, ever-elusive tribute and testament to the really, really, well-lived life.

And what we do for clients, be they modernists or traditionalists, and whether they seek an architecture of foreground or background, resembles coaching more than anything else. Once we truly understand a client's program and purpose, we can then exuberantly and rigorously design a home that listens rather than lectures, and one that can evolve and grow: slowly, over time.

# Saving the Family Cottage in Reverse

I've been afforded a life of privilege, mostly through the generosity of others. I've been invited by countless friends, starting in high school, to visit and stay with them in their families' second homes. As a post-graduate living in New York City, I began to think of myself as America's favorite guest. Rhetorically, how could friends enjoy their large vacation homes if they did not bring their materially less fortunate friends. All the better, if the guests could ski, golf, play tennis, or even just favor sitting fireside or on a dock working the Sunday crossword puzzle.

As residential architects, we often find ourselves studying multigenerational homes and finding ways to preserve birthright homes for future generations. When designing anew, we ask whether the home will become a gathering place for the owners, their children, and grandchildren—whether imminent or years down the road. When evaluating renovations and additions to existing homes, we immediately ask whether a succession plan is in place. Most homes that families have enjoyed for many years, decades, and even centuries, desperately need functional updating and are burdened with nearly incalculable deferred maintenance. The costs, therefore, of passing a home from one generation to the next presents significant challenges. Most multigenerational homes were built by forebears who built for their immediate family, without much thought of the wants and needs of grandchildren and great grandchildren who would follow.

Evolving from favored guest to estate planning advisor was seamless.

Some forty years ago, I was snowed in at a high school friend's ski house in Northern Michigan, and in a seeming blink of an eye, I am a forty-year-old celebrating Memorial Day on Millionaire's Row in Bolton Landing, NY, just across the lake from the famed Sagamore Hotel. Over several visits, I became very familiar with the "Big House" on Lake George's Mohican Point inhabited by the fourth and fifth generation offspring of the home's builder. Today, some 120 descendants share the house and property, including the oldest boat on the lake, an original ELCO (Electric Boat Company) runabout that debuted at the Columbian Exposition in Chicago in 1893. The "Big Man" who built the Palladian manse called the "Big House" for his growing family at the turn of the 19th century, was named William Bixby, a Saint Louis railway man (robber baron) with seven children (six daughters). Like other multigenerational families, the descendants all differ in their connection to the home— geographically and spiritually—as well as in their ability to afford supporting a second home with ongoing repairs and operating expenses. Many years after his death, The Big Man's heirs reconfigured the home, creating six apartments, one for each enduring branch of the family. Today the apartments, common areas, accessory dwellings, boathouse, and boats are all managed by a family board, and the multigenerational heart beats on.

Wondering whether others had approached the succession problem similarly to the "Big House" with its multigenerational board, I sought out a book entitled *Saving the Family Cottage: A Guide to Succession Planning for your Cottage, Cabin, Camp, or Vacation Home* by Stuart Hollander, David Fry, and Rose Hollander (2013). I keep multiple copies on my office shelf, ready to share with friends and family looking to "save the family cottage." To be fair, the book written by Northern Michigan lawyers is not an easy read, but it coherently and compellingly describes the conundrum of succession planning and sets forth a legal framework to help families resolve their different needs and maintain ownership and enjoyment of their family heritage.

Unfortunately, the "Big House" on Mohican Point is something of an outlier today. More often than not, the family homestead built a century or more ago comes under an insurmountable assault due to estate taxes, deferred maintenance, sibling rivalries (or worse), and varying needs.

Without adequate planning, the original acreage is sold, the roof begins to leak, and with each passing season, family members take to sitting around the porch with the broken rail telling and retelling ever taller tales of days gone by, while brokers trudge through with their phalanx of potential buyers, most of whom are deaf and blind to the family's weepy reminiscences.

In his 2004 book, *The Big House, a Century in the Life of an American Summer Home*, George Colt poignantly writes about his family home on Cape Cod that could not be saved from the march of time and succumbs to the passage of time. I could not put the book down and not just because of its familiar title, as the story so perfectly matches that of many of the multigenerational piles (yes, that is an architectural term), that so gloriously dominate our oceansides, lakesides, and rolling hills.

While we have tried on several occasions to design and provide programmatic solutions to "save the family cottage," we often find we have been brought in a little too late, and the aggregate challenges win out. With all this visiting, thinking, and reading, I got to wondering, what would saving the family cottage look like in reverse?

I realized we have begun exploring this idea with three different families, two of whom are extended family and the other, friends of many years. I find this especially exciting, as I thoroughly enjoy working with friends and family. The first study, barely just begun, is for cousins, who are ten years older than I and have three adult children and a first grandchild and (hopefully) more to come. They are considering building a new home in the country as a family gathering place, a brand new multigenerational "Big House." We are finding as we sit down with this program in mind, we are designing in a new paradigm. Instead of converting an existing estate to the needs of children and grandchildren, we are conceiving spaces where no memories will exist of the "room in which I grew up." No spouses will be sleeping on a child's twin bed surrounded by primary and high school awards, certificates, medals, and trophies. Perhaps this new home will have three or four discrete suites or wings, one for each young family and with a central kitchen and living spaces – both indoor and outdoor. The parents' primary bedroom will certainly be on the ground floor, yet far enough from the communal space for privacy, both physical and acoustic.

The second case study closely resembles the first, except the parents are in their early fifties and younger than most empty-nesters contemplating building their forever home. Their four sons range in age from high school to post-collegiate, and no spouses or grandchildren in the immediate future. Still, they have bought eight acres with spectacular views and are beginning to plan for a home in the exact way as the first family. Should we split the necessary bedrooms between two structures, a main house and a pool house, and should they be built at the same time or over time? Should the primary be on the second floor to capture the view, and if so, shouldn't there still be a downstairs primary for when they get older? How will the house mature as the family dynamics evolve?

The final project is for my wife's cousins, who having retired, thought to modestly improve their weekend home for themselves and for the kids and grandkids. Our first conversations focused on small renovations and improvements. By the time we finished the programming discussions, we collectively concluded the most appropriate strategy would be to significantly reimagine the house from foundation to roof, tackling deferred maintenance and replacing legacy building systems as we go. Working largely within the existing footprint, we plan to build a new house that will function for the next generation and beyond. This means a primary bedroom on the first floor, with children and grandchildren residing upstairs, with en suite bathrooms, a family room to congregate and a large bunk room. The walk-out basement will have billiards and ping pong, as well as pool changing rooms and baths. At the end of the day, the home will not be spectacularly unusual, but it will extend the family's enjoyment of the home for at least a generation, if not longer.

We find we are tackling estate planning in two profound ways. First, we are designing homes that will joyfully accommodate and embrace generational transitions and continuity. It turns out the empty-nest home may need to be larger than the house in which the kids were raised. "If you build it, they will come," *Field of Dreams (1989)* sums it up well. At the same time, we are providing a second more conventional form of estate planning: financial estate planning for parents with adult children who have wherewithal to pass on to the next generation(s). If one is building for the next 100 years, not for a return-on-investment, the imperatives of short term economic priorities and resale value are replaced with objectives of a much longer duration. Approached in this manner, the family estate becomes the very foundation of financial estate planning. Why not pass on to the children and grandchildren the family gathering place many, many years before the inevitable; even better if a trust is set up to pay for decades of property taxes and ongoing maintenance. I contend the strategies set forth in "Saving the Family Cottage" are equally operative when the house is yet to be built, in that the generational stakeholders can all participate in the location scouting, programming and design of the project. Nothing seems more rewarding and prudent than using shelter as an effective inheritance tax shelter and long-term financial plan. It is time to call the accountant, the lawyer, and the real estate broker—and, of course, the architect.

# Columns are Our Friends

In the mid-seventies, theorist and architect Peter Eisenman designed a modest modern house in Cornwall, Connecticut. The home had many peculiar elements: an upside-down staircase on which no one could travel; a narrow, floor-to-ceiling window dividing the headboard wall of the primary bedroom thwarting the installation of a queen or king bed; a "column" that hovered over the kitchen island and clearly had no structural purpose; and a structural column situated precisely where one of the chairs around a dining room table should reside. By all accounts, the owners who commissioned the home lived quite happily in Eisenman's work of art and enjoyed the daily confrontation of having the architect quite literally present at the dinner table during every meal.

While I believe each of our former clients would welcome me as a dinner guest, I cannot think of one who would accept my columnar avatar in lieu of one of their dining room chairs.

At DFA, as at most successful residential architecture firms, one of our key design objectives is to never intentionally compromise the functionality of a home. Challenges are, however, an inevitable part of every design and construction endeavor. When I look back on completed projects, I find that success is the direct result of conflicts and limitations that were overcome. Solutions that satisfy complex and competing needs have a depth and refinement that might have been missed if we were given unlimited resources—space, time, and funds. Demanding that a space satisfy more than one programmatic function inevitably provides design opportunities, and successful designs represent the nuanced resolution of complicated, challenging, and often conflicting conditions.

I found this to be especially true when designing a home for my family. We were considering buying a house in foreclosure. It was in bad shape; it had an 18th century portion and a series of 20th century additions and would require wholesale renovation and restoration. Nervous about the upcoming transaction, I invited a dear friend (and multi-time client) to visit the house with me. During our walk around the property, I lamented that I could not see a way forward, only insurmountable challenges. He said he'd never heard me admit I couldn't envision an exciting path. He urged me to overcome my hesitation and proceed with the purchase. He was certain, he said, that I would have an "epiphanic" moment.

Two or three nights later, that moment occurred. Suddenly, I could visualize the form the house would take. The details have since evolved, but the house which we now enjoy is very close in form and substance to the one I envisioned after having been so challenged at the onset.

In Manhattan, we often uncover surprises behind walls. Ideally, we find them at the very beginning of a project, while we are still surveying a space and creating the precise and measured drawings upon which we base our designs. Inevitably, however, there are times when surprises are uncovered during demolition or later. The urgent design adjustments that result often have considerable impact. No one—not us, not the contractors, and certainly not the clients—embraces these discoveries with enthusiasm. Yet, we have learned to take a deep breath and evaluate the situation with as much rigor and impartiality as we can muster.

Over the years, we have gained confidence from our experience handling surprises, and are able to reassure ourselves—and our panicked and wary clients—that all will be okay. In fact, better than okay.

At one Monday morning meeting, I presented the account you've just read. That very afternoon, the exact situation arose: demolition on an apartment project uncovered a large structural column that was not shown on our architectural plans. Even though this column was hidden behind sheetrock, it should have appeared in our surveys. To make matters worse, the offending column was in area intended as open space. Once we overcame our embarrassment and dismay, we took stock and began sketching. The column was located just outside the kitchen, so we came to the idea of adding a large, semicircular dining alcove and banquette at one side of it and utilizing the back side as additional pantry space. Once constructed, the alcove became a beautiful feature of the home, and over time, became one of the homeowner's favorite and most utilized parts of the apartment.

While we don't seek surprises and would never intentionally foist one on a client, we have found that the new ideas they generate are often preferable to the original. Our confidence in these outcomes sometimes prompts skepticism from clients ("But I don't *want* a column in the middle of my kitchen!") and even fury ("*How* did you miss this?!?") And yet once completed, and once the home is more beautiful than originally envisioned, we can't help but conclude that, indeed, "Columns are our Friends."

# Some People Hate Walnut

In describing our work, we often use words like "timeless" and "universal," setting forth that design preferences are more similar than different. During the early design phases, we frequently but erroneously believe we have presented something unique and special, only to run across something strikingly similar in person, online, or in a magazine. We both set trends and succumb to trend-following. We are arbiters of style and most of the time our team shares a common sensibility. Our clients, on the other hand, have tastes and preferences that are comparatively diverse. Navigating between the current themes and aesthetics preferred by our team and each client's sensibilities and associations is a dynamic and fluid process. Successful projects stem from this collaboration and integration, and the more carefully we listen to and incorporate a client's wants and needs, the better the result.

Listening should be easier than it is. Because we are retained to lead and to express our opinions, careful listening is not explicitly expected – and yet, it is without question our priority. I rarely make it through a week without reminding clients that we are designing their home, not our own. If anyone wishes to see how I choose to live, visit danielfrisch.com and pull up the pictures of "Kent Hollow" or "Dan's Books." I am confident that many of our clients would like to live in such a wonderful house, but I am equally certain that none should. Thousands of decisions go into the design of a home, and while certain projects may share design DNA, every home is unique. This individualization intimidates some, and that which should be fun and exciting can instead be overwhelming. For more on this, please see the chapter "The Tyranny of Too Much" about having too many decisions to make. As we lead clients through the design process, we try to balance our expertise and passions with theirs, while also streamlining the decisions. Clients wouldn't need us if they could design their own homes, and equally true, we would have few homes to design without patrons.

Early in the programming phase of a project, we work closely with our clients to understand the project drivers, everything from budget, function, and aesthetics. In working with clients on their program, we go far below the surface. The initial questions are many. How many bedrooms? A first-floor primary? Is an open kitchen preferred? How often will the owner entertain? If we were to formulate a questionnaire, the most basic questions would number in the hundreds. To make matters more challenging, spouses and children (when they are involved in project planning) often disagree about priorities and project specifics. Once the functional program is outlined, we seek to understand the aesthetic program. No matter the challenges of expression, anyone undertaking a project has strong pre-formed ideas about what their ideal home should look like. While we find geographic, socioeconomic, and generational similarities to be shared by many, we know enough to know not to assume we know a client's aesthetic program based on superficial assessments. Working with a combination of saved Houzz images and Pinterest boards, clients have come to abandon the "I know it when I see it" method of communication, and instead to come to initial meetings armed with collections of images. Once we begin to understand the functional and aesthetic program, we can compare these collected thoughts to the project budget, the third element of a nuanced and developed project program.

Reaching an understanding of the major program items usually comes easily, and preliminary plans take shape with clarity and enthusiasm. As designs are refined and as final decisions are made, and even more significantly, as construction commences, it is natural for clients to second-guess certain decisions about which they had been previously resolute. When going through this inevitable process of reconsideration, we've found our clients fall into two camps: the ninety percent that comfortably reaffirm their choices and the ten percent who, with great embarrassment and even unhappiness, ask for a change. Studying these metrics always reminds me of a specific Psychology 101 lecture class in college, when our professor introduced us to the concept of cognitive dissonance. The segment of the course was based on the work of Leon Festinger's *A Theory of Cognitive Dissonance* (1962). Dr. Festinger lays out the dispute between head and heart at the very basis of design decision-making. Dissonance, according to Festinger, comes when your intellect or heart wants one thing but your heart or intellect argues for the opposite. Working with and reconciling this dissonance is a daily process for those of us who lead design teams and interact with clients.

We are aided in our navigation by the ninety-ten rule, as I've termed it. Ninety percent of the time a reconsideration is resolved in favor of the original decision. This is a happy occurrence as reconsiderations invariably arrive at awkward times—often after construction has commenced or when installations are complete. Reconsiderations that occur mid-construction are particularly vexing as incomplete construction only affords a partial image of a completed composition. Our job is to help complete the picture and aid our clients in understanding whether the design will weather the crisis in confidence and whether we should move forward without significant redesign. As Dr. Festinger observed, most dissonance is resolved in the favor of the original selection. Provided enough work and diligence went into the original decision, the mind settles on the first preference as not being subjective (or dissonant) but rather as resolute and objective. This process of careful consideration leading to selections helps explain why opinions are held with such consistency in all manner of subjective categories – from music (who is your favorite band?) to sports teams (ask a Wolverine fan how he or she feels about Ohio State), or politics (no parentheticals needed). Very few people waver or display any real dissonance or willingness to reconsider when it comes to such dug-in subjects.

When commissioning a home, most clients lack this level of certainty, and hesitation and disagreements appear with great predictability. While most design conflicts are readily resolved, the occasional reconsideration presages an actual change rather than an affirmation. No matter how carefully criteria are considered on paper, and no matter the certainty of conviction, dissonance creeps in and people change their minds. On most occasions, communication—or lack thereof—is blamed as the culprit. While communication can always be better, most changes are the result of unknown dissonance, based on conditions or circumstances lurking below the surface and not discernable during earlier conversations. Confusing twenty-twenty hindsight with a lack of initial vision is a danger, leading directly to blame and recrimination. When inevitable changes arise, we find it better to embrace the new direction, especially as our ninety-ten rule suggests that an out-of-the-blue reconsideration is a relatively unusual circumstance.

Extensive and intimate programming conversations seek to reduce the likelihood of dissonance, and our awareness of the concept helps us to anticipate concerns that may arise. Notwithstanding, we are periodically surprised by a client reaction to a particular installation. On one such occasion, we saw an opportunity to utilize a small area of leftover space within a wall of a client's entry hall. Thinking we would deliver a pleasant surprise to our client, we designed a walnut art niche that elegantly capitalized upon the found space. The happy event was undercut by the client's immediate statement when the surprise installation was unveiled—she expressed that she HATED walnut. It is quite possible that this was shared during early conversations, but I'll never know for sure. Tastes and preferences vary, sometimes greatly, and beauty as they say is in the eye of the beholder. Today, the offending walnut niche is painted a lovely shade of white and all is right with the world.

# Playing Extra Holes

*The effect of "scope creep" on budget.*

The successful navigation of budgets and schedules is a cornerstone of rewarding relationships. To maintain transparency and accuracy, we base our budget recommendations on a historical analysis of the actual expenditures of comparable projects. We use the same process to estimate project durations. Each project we complete provides additional data and makes us better forecasters, and we include budget and schedule discussions in our earliest consultations.

Yet, even with rigorous estimating, project budgets and timelines often expand, and meaningfully so. Numerous factors contribute to budget overruns and delays, with the number one catalyst being "scope creep," both during the design phases, and post-construction commencement. Our eyes always seem to be larger than our stomachs, at least when it comes to managing budgets. While thorough architectural plans form the basis for the preparation of pre-construction estimates for construction, they cannot anticipate program additions post-construction commencement. Projects predictably evolve and costs often increase, and schedules extend. We keep a running tally of post-construction commencement increases (change orders), and our projects average an increase of twelve to fourteen percent after construction has begun. Unbelievably, we are proud of this record when discussing and comparing industry norms with our colleagues. Setting aside whether this is an accomplishment or signifies a lack of discipline, our data supports the universality of "scope creep".

Not surprisingly, clients receive reports of significant cost escalations and schedule extensions with the opposite of enthusiasm. While ten percent (plus) escalations and reasonable schedule extensions are anticipated, many projects escalate further and schedules drag on. Even when costs accrete based on additive work and more expensive material selections, frustrated clients demand explanations and look to blame. Contractors feel underappreciated, and architects move into damage-control mode trying to explain why the "goal posts have moved." While I like the football reference, I prefer the more appropriate analogy from golf that the client has elected to "play extra holes." An established budget is very similar to a golf course's par and difficulty (slope) rating. In theory, a scratch golfer can play the course in an allotted number of strokes, or "par." The rest of us will take more strokes than par and carry handicap indexes that establish our individual par expectation by adding strokes to the printed scorecard. Metaphorically, construction contracts establish a project's par, and every contractor invoice tracks performance relative to the stated par. As construction costs increase due to scope creep, this par should be adjusted as if one had elected to play additional holes.

Exacerbating the frustration is the contractor's understanding that clients will be frustrated and distrustful when costs escalate. Contractors are often hesitant to fully document that client requests (as well as site conditions, bidding errors, and material and labor cost increases) have occasioned costs to rise, effectively lengthening the course, often by many holes. Contractor timidity is understandable since this information is usually shared at the time of invoicing and contractors fear that payments will be negotiated or withheld. Instead of resetting par for the course, they try to accommodate an increase in scope while maintaining the original cost estimate and schedule, effectively kicking the can down the road. This attempt to skirt confrontation invariably fails, as costs are real, and an honest assessment of changes (increases) is unavoidable. Clients need to realize in real time the impact of decisions and discoveries if they are expected to embrace a redefined project budget and schedule.

As relationship managers, it is our role to reassure builders and owners that cost escalations and schedule extensions are not failures; they are the necessary result of definable circumstances and additional scope requests. One arrow in our quiver is to recharacterize scope creep from unsettling "change orders" to "additional work authorizations." While this distinction may seem semantic, a more affirmative reaction to additional work is palpable. So much so, that we are working to remove entirely the term "change order" from our vocabulary.

Evaluating budget and schedule performance with accuracy only occurs when comparing increased costs and schedule extensions to an increased par. While this sounds simple, resetting par is contrary to the emotional fabric and institutional history of construction. Clients are always frustrated by cost escalations and schedule extensions and look for accountability - too often in the wrong place. Contractors and architects want happy, not discouraged, clients and want to deliver on their original promises. "We build on time and on budget" is the hallmark of every successful architect and builder. It is not spin when we validate the concept of on-time, on-budget delivery, as long as the budgets and time frames are properly reset to match the invariable scope creep that occurs.

It serves the best interest of all parties to recognize that playing extra holes is not only OK, but it can also be done with enthusiasm. Let's tee it up and enjoy a third nine.

# The Tyranny of Too Much

In 2004, Barry Schwartz wrote a book titled *The Paradox of Choice : Why More is Less* (2004), and one Monday morning many years later, our team watched him deliver a Ted Talk Video on the subject.

Mr. Schwartz addresses the depression that develops from the first-world abundance of everyday choices, in everything from salad dressing to blue jeans.

We've discovered the same dilemma presents itself in residential design. Whether we are studying a layout, selecting bathroom tile, or even simply picking a light fixture, we are bombarded with options. Rarely is one choice fully preferable, and when interconnected with other elements, clear and decisive design can be elusive. When getting dressed, people often ask "does this go together?" Imagine going through this decision-making process for hundreds of elements in a home, all the while knowing the selections have a certain permanence. To make matters worse, decisions often seem equally weighted and it can become difficult to differentiate between and balance primary, secondary, and tertiary decisions.

While *The Paradox of Choice* provides insights into modern society and the consequences of abundant choice, the book doesn't provide a particularly specific tool kit for our daily endeavors. Dan Graham, my tenth-grade mechanical drawing teacher, however, taught us the K.I.S.S. method, "Keep It Simple, Stupid." I've enjoyed studying and refining our design process, and love when we come across the work of a writer like Barry Schwartz or recall an influential teacher like Dan Graham who reinforce and remind us of our commitment to our fundamental principles of design.

We rigorously implement these lessons, regardless of project scope or complexity. For even the largest and most complicated projects, we begin by outlining and clarifying project priorities, thereby refining the "program" for the project. At each stage of development, we continue to find ways to simplify the parameters and to make design decisions with greater clarity.

For the last decade, we've focused on the K.I.S.S. method, and on using *The Paradox of Choice* as a base platform, and have begun to offer clients with more modest projects a pre-selected palate of materials. By limiting the decision making, we deliver a streamlined process, improving budgets and schedules, and most importantly, allowing clients to prioritize the larger and more primary decisions. Over the years, we've found that our simpler projects with greater limitations are as creative and successful as our larger commissions.

It takes great discipline to tune out superfluous variables and an overabundance of choices. Finding a balance between "less is more" and "more is more" is a worthy goal.

# Wait, What... White?

On October 7, 2015, the Benjamin Moore Company announced that it was naming OC-117 "Simply White" its 2016 Color of the Year. The press release described white as "a timeless and versatile design statement," as well as "transcendent, powerful, and polarizing—it is either taken for granted or obsessed over." Ellen O'Neill, Benjamin Moore's creative director, added, "White is not just a design trend, it is a design essential. The popularity of white, the necessity of white, the mystique of white is quantifiable in our history." While it is possible to quantify popularity by analyzing sales data, I can't imagine how Benjamin Moore went about quantifying the ephemeral mystique of white.

After the announcement, an online debate raged between design purists who embraced the essential nature of white and color advocates who insisted Benjamin Moore had selected no color at all as its Color of the Year. Perhaps this fight might have been avoided if Benjamin Moore had selected a white with a more colorful name, like OC-65 "Chantilly Lace," described thus in the catalogue: "Delicate and refined as the lace it was named after, this crisp, clean white evokes images of pure silk, soft linen and simpler times." Since "Chantilly Lace" is almost indistinguishable from "Simply White", I assume Benjamin Moore knew exactly what it was doing in selecting the latter as its Color of the Year. The marketing team must have been ecstatic about the ensuing emperor's-new-clothes dispute, until, as fate would have it, a backlash occurred. Was "Simply White" a racial slur, as some people insisted?

We residential designers discuss paint—white and otherwise—a great deal. Our clients invariably find paint and paint preparation costs exorbitant, while painting subcontractors maintain that labor costs threaten profitability. Both assessments are true, not unlike the paradoxical assertion that white paint can be both taken for granted and obsessed over. Of all the construction trades, painting's economics are distinguished by being predominantly labor. The materials are comparatively inexpensive, and moreover, those labor expenses are mostly accrued in the unseen work of preparation.

Paint and spackle alone won't disguise a problematic wall surface. To achieve a top-quality, high-end paint job, wall surfaces must first be skim-coated, whereby a coat of plaster is applied to the wall surface, allowed to dry, fully sanded and brushed clean, after which the process is repeated—many times over. A level-five skim coat calls for this process to be repeated a minimum of five times until the walls are glass-smooth. During the final stages of a project, the air on the job site becomes saturated with fine white dust particles and laborers emerge at the end of the day looking as if they've been coated head to toe in confectioner's sugar.

Specialty paint effects require particular preparation and additional coats of paint and drive costs. So do certain boutique paint brands, such as those made by the English company Farrow and Ball. Unlike Benjamin Moore, Farrow & Ball (F&B) offers a limited, constantly curated selection of 132 colours. The British spelling encourages F&B acolytes to speak with a British lilt, and the brand mystique is reinforced by the "intriguing story behind each colour name." Marketing aside, the brand has built its reputation on the quality of its paint; adherents claim F&B paints offer a greater depth of color than competitors' offerings. When New York City painters first began using F&B, they expected the formulations to be superior, and the lay-up and coverage far better than that of the domestic competition. While this may be true in the hands of some experienced painters, others found the opposite and now charge not only for the higher cost of the paint itself but also for the additional coats required to achieve a quality finish.

When a client is a steadfast fan of a particular paint company or specialty finish, we enthusiastically support their choice and specify boutique paints and processes. Rarely are we disappointed with the results, even when my personal choices might have differed. With clients who go this route, we generally opt not to share a favorite SNL skit, in which Aidy Bryant, an "out-of-work day bartender," defends her choice to invest her inheritance in F&B "colooours" because she refuses to live in "squalooour."

For my purposes, I have adopted the Henry Ford Model T approach: I like any color, as long as it's white. I also espouse that I would rather spend my money on art than on painting the walls. Why spend exorbitant sums on preparation and paint when the hope is to cover them in art? While I am glad the patrons of Michelangelo and Tintoretto felt otherwise, I prefer my art to be portable and not permanently fused with the walls.

For the prix fixe DFA Studio Program we picked a Benjamin Moore white, OC-59 "Vanilla Milkshake," as our standard color. We came across "Vanilla Milkshake" when trying to precisely match the color of naked plaster (joint compound) used in skim coating. Of all the Benjamin Moore whites and off-whites, "Vanilla Milkshake" has no discernable hue—not yellow, green, blue or pink—nor does not it look like an overly brilliant "art studio" white.

While Benjamin Moore offers more than 150 whites and off-whites and an estimated 3500 colors in total, Farrow and Ball's total color line never wavers from 132 colors; the company retires one when another is introduced. Following the premise of *The Paradox of Choice*, I believe Benjamin Moore could significantly reduce its white and off-white offerings without compromising aesthetic possibilities. Yet to many Americans, the whole idea of choice feels like luxury. Color wars are no longer the realm of sleep-away camps and street gangs. Paint has become a status symbol.

When it came time to paint the walls inside our Connecticut home, I joked with our painter that I wanted just white and not a color named "Just

White," or "Simply White," or "Super White." After the resulting Abbott and Costello routine, I did a little research and found to my surprise that Benjamin Moore actually offers a color named "White." What an easy pick. I now live in a "White" house and a "White" apartment, baffling people who might have expected me to choose a color with a more romantic moniker. "Wait—what? *White*?" always makes me think of "Who's on First?" And, oh yeah, "What's on Second," and "I Dunno is on Third."

# Ode to Butter Board

During the COVID-19 pandemic, we fared better than most. We design private homes in the city and the country for clients who came to realize that "home" had become more important than ever. We are nimble and small, and forward-looking. Even so, our personal and professional lives were affected in many ways, and—probably permanently. Our office was dark from March through September 2020, with our team collaborating with clients, contractors, and consultants over FaceTime and Zoom. When we reopened the office that fall, any day would find a population of two, three, or four of us in residence, re-engaging, but lacking the energy we've always enjoyed. Once it was prudent and safe for us to come back together as a full group, we made a few changes. We embraced schedule flexibility, including the adoption of Remote Fridays, perhaps the most popular decision in the firm's history.

Technology has both enabled remote collaboration and altered our space needs. Forgotten are the outsized drafting tables, mechanical pencils, electric erasers, mylar sheets, and stacks of large format blueprints. Although architects may be among the last to go fully paperless, we now require less space and we muse about our office of the future. How much space do we really need? Should we sublet a floor (half our space) to a strategic partner? Should we relocate entirely? One fantasy has us leasing a *Mad Men* space on a high floor of a midtown skyscraper, jettisoning stuff as if Marie Kondo were our in-house office coach. Wouldn't it feel cathartic to discard the accumulated clutter, everything from the legacy job files to the outdated catalogues which fill our every nook and cranny? And, if we were to downsize or relocate, what do we value most and what would we bring along?

Thinking about our office needs and answering the question of what we value most has been cathartic. Without question, our greatest assets are our people and our culture; but as we have proven during the pandemic, we can keep the team together by adapting and utilizing technology. While most of our collected "stuff" could be stored off site or discarded, there are things we would miss. The furniture in my office is very special to me: the steel surfboard-shaped conference table was designed by an artist for our original narrow conference room back in 1993 and the chairs are vintage mid-century swivelers in a shade of brick red that I never thought I would like, much less come to love. My oversize 'firesafe' faux-woodgrain steel desk came from a tire dealer in Texas and cost more to ship than to purchase. In one of the rooms is an impressive 1950s Italian bar cabinet with exquisite chevron marquetry designed by Vittorio Dassi. As we assess both value and nostalgic importance, the few pieces of furniture rate highly, but can't compare to our books and art. Our design library has curated volumes that I have collected since I first fell in love with architecture during high school. I am sure we could replace the books, but I doubt I would have the heart to do so. We reference these volumes on a near-daily basis, and while everything is available today on the worldwide web, nothing compares to pulling down an old favorite and sharing it with a colleague.

Next, and growing in sentimental value, is the art hanging throughout the office. Almost every piece has been created by a friend, many for whom we've hung shows and celebrated at our annual holiday parties. Each work has a story, and each is irreplaceable, no less to us than if they had been painted by the modern masters. One of the great disappointments of 2020 was that we had to cancel that year's holiday party and we could not hang a planned show for a dear friend and artist from Puerto Rico whose work we favor.

Collectively, the furniture, books, and art are extremely valuable to us and meaningfully contribute to our identity. As special as these items may be, they do not compare to the items we create ourselves. The objects I cherish most are the in-house scale models we make of each home we design. Architects have always made physical models out of chip board, plastic and bass wood, and more recently utilizing CNC machines, laser-cutters, and 3-D printers. We also now rely on realistic computer renderings to help our clients and contractors visualize and for our team to refine design propositions. Notwithstanding, I have a well-earned reputation as a dinosaur, and I insist that we make our own in-house physical models. We use X-acto knives, straight edges, and a particular yellowish paper board with a high rag content called "butter-board."

We've made models since the day we opened, and the butter board house models started in 1997, when we were awarded our first commission to design a ground-up home. Our firm was young—as was I—and while we were convinced we had a viable composition, we did not know for sure until we got out the butter-board, straight edges, and knives and made our model. Twenty-plus years later, this early model sits prominently on a bar cart across from my desk as a daily reminder that simple tools can be very effective in solving complex challenges.

Almost anywhere you look in the office you'll see butter-board models, from small massing models to cut-away studies of brownstones and intricate stair assemblies. One weekend in the early aughts, I received a near-panicky call from clients who were seeing their stair in person for the first time. The stair connecting two apartments in a landmarked Gramercy co-operative was designed as a graceful and delicate curving stair floating in front of two stories of windows. Upon installation, the clients were certain that the stair had been installed backwards, as if the architect or fabricator suffered from dyslexia. Concerned, I took a Sunday evening cab to the office, picked up the butter-board model, and took another cab down to the clients' apartment. Sure enough, the model perfectly matched the installed staircase, and we were able to communicate why the stair could only work as configured. Today, the model is a little worse for wear, but every time I come across it in the office, I chuckle.

After reopening, we began a model for a house design and when we checked stock, we realized we were running a bit low on butter-board, and sadly, Midtown sources no longer exist. With computer-aided design (CAD) replacing hand drawing and model making, there is less and less of a call for these supplies. Charrette, Sam Flax, and Lee's Art Shop have all closed. In December of 2020, our blueprinter on Madison Avenue succumbed and turned off their plotters and printers for the last time. Blick Art Supplies, just north of NYU, had a box of forty sheets of butter-board which we snapped up, even though the color was inconsistent. An internet search informed us that the manufacturer, Alvin Drafting, LLC (founded 1950) discontinued the product and is going through a re-structuring, promising to reopen with a smaller, more carefully curated offering of drafting tools and materials. This begs the question, how many forty-sheet boxes of discontinued 30" x 40" butter board should we buy for future use? I have a hunch we are about to corner the market.

Not counting all the study and detail models, we have on display in the office a dozen individual models of our ground-up homes. The houses have been built in Michigan, Virginia, New Hampshire, New York, Vermont, and Connecticut, and while the location, program, style, and scale are all unique, the one element that has been consistent has been the butter-board. All things being equal, our clients get the satisfaction and profound enjoyment of living in their dream homes, and we get to keep the models. And, in that *Mad Men* office of our dreams, I picture a spotlit gallery with nothing but stark white pedestals and Lucite-boxed butter-board models.

*Note: A couple of years later, Utrecht once again is selling butter board, and for the foreseeable future we will have material on hand to make models for new commissions.*

# SkySpace Lech

This is my first post that can fairly be called a dispatch – I started it on my laptop in the library of the Gasthof Rote Wand in Lech, Austria, while enjoying Spring Break 2019 with my family, as well as with Jamie who has worked with us at DFA for the better part of three decades. Between ski runs, meals, and pool time, Jamie and I are able to talk quietly, considering DFA from a distance, and we share insights and thoughts without the distractions of the day-to-day. The trip is made even more special as Jamie's father's family is Austrian, and he has generations of family in Lech.

Austria is a long way to travel, but Jamie, his wife, Zoe, and their extended family—we stay in a cousin's hotel—welcome us and make us feel at home. Lech is an Alpen ski-resort community with a full-time population of only 1500, yet boasting 8500 hotel beds. Perhaps my favorite thing about the area, other than it being the birthplace of alpine skiing, is that the families who owned most of the property before resort days built the hotels, ski lifts, and resort amenities and maintain them to this day. Sheraton, Hilton, Ritz Carlton and the Four Seasons brands are nowhere to be found. In the 1990s when Jamie first started telling me about Lech and its tradition of hospitality, design, and architecture, I thought he was simply up-selling his ancestral home. I know people from Grand Rapids (my childhood home) to Charlotte (a recently visited place) who do the same thing. I believe all places deserve such pride of place, but notwithstanding, Jamie is right—Lech is spectacular.

Architecturally, I'll limit myself to a hotel and two restaurants we've come to know very well. The first is Walch's Rote Wand Gourmethotel in the hamlet of Zug on the perimeter of Lech. The Rote Wand is owned and run by Jamie's cousin Joschi and his wife Natasha. The main building's address is Zug 5, as it is the fifth oldest structure in Zug, dating to the 16th century. The building is un-presupposing from the exterior, appearing similar to many—if not most— of the snow-covered, shallow pitched structures throughout Lech. The Rote Wand commenced operations as a Gasthof in 1959, and was at the time on the forefront of traditional Austrian design and hospitality. Today, when walking through the hotel, recently and ingeniously re-branded as a "Gourmet Hotel", I am struck by the simple and graceful modernity of the lobby, bar, and dining room with their clean lines, warm natural oak paneling, and subtle elegant lighting. The public spaces of the Rote Wand are more akin to Alvar Aalto and Scandinavian Classicism than what one might expect inside a 400 year-old vernacular building in the Alps. The modern themes continue to the guest rooms and suites each featuring unique layouts and spa-like materials.

Two restaurants we visit every trip are separated by a single chair lift, yet are a world apart. The first is in town at the base of the Schlegelkopf lift, and the second is 2500 meters above sea level at the top of the same lift. The in-town restaurant is named Schneggarei, and from the outside, it is looks like any other Lech building. Inside, the blend of modernity and vernacular is so seamless that the casual observer and patron might miss the countless subtle design innovations. If one were to aspire to create architecture that recedes into the background yet still delights, I would be hard-pressed to present a better example than the restaurant Schneggarei.

After we grab our skis and get on the lifts and, as we reach the summit of Petersboden high above Lech, a building comes into view. It looks deceptively like a modern utility barn, perhaps one that would house the sno-cats that roam the mountain each evening. But, as we ski from the lift over to the structure, we come upon Der Wolf, a restaurant that captures and enhances a view as well as any I have ever encountered. There are other panoramic restaurants above Lech, one or two of which hang precariously over the Alpine edge, but none justify our annual trip in the same way as Der Wolf. I have taken pictures of it, through it, and from it and I can't do it justice. I've even taken out my pen and sketched it, not that I had a prayer of capturing it's essence, but that I might study it a bit more carefully and by doing so, remember it a bit more clearly.

Clarity brings me to the primary subject of this dispatch: James Turrell's SkySpace. As a contemporary artist, James Turrell has contributed significantly to our understanding of light, architecture, and nature, and I've been an admirer of his work since graduate school. The residents of Lech, all 1500 of them, sought out James Turrell to conceive and install a permanent work of art in nature showcasing their pride of place. The result is SkySpace Lech, one of ninety-something SkySpaces Mr. Turrell has erected in places of resplendent natural beauty around the world. We talked the kids into joining us for the walk up the hill and when we arrived at the smallish oval structure in the biting cold, I'd thought we had made a mistake in pushing our art tour upon them. But after half an hour of playing in the snow high in the Alps, the frigid children and parents settled in for a fifteen-minute "tour" of the SkySpace. As the sun set in the perfect oval room with its crisply cut oculus open to the sky, and as the domed space changed colors (or was the sky changing?), even our nine and seven-year old kids became transfixed. At Der Wolf, the spectacular framing of the Alps is supplemented, depending on age, by schnapps and French fries. In James Turrell's SkyScape, there is nothing besides the precise manipulation of light and nature to compel reflection and to awe. Old and young were awed in spite of the chill, until we struggled to pull ourselves away and to walk back down the mountain to the comfort of our home at the Rote Wand. Thank you to the 1500 residents of Lech who had the vision and wherewithal to commission James Turrell and to bring SkySpace to Lech. While it is a very small structure, it's vision is as vast as its setting in the limitless Alpine landscape.

I finished typing this on our return flight to New York, having enjoyed such abundance, I was left with only one question. Why do airlines not serve kids' meals?

Note: During spring break of 2024, we returned to Lech and on a perfect March evening, I took a couple to visit Skyspace. I again was awed, as were they, and I am already looking forward to returning. In 2023, James Turrell installed a Skyspace on the roof of the Friends Seminary School in downtown Manhattan. No matter how tough the tickets are to come by, it is a much shorter commute than to Lech, and we will get there soon enough.

*James Turrell, Skyspace Lech, Oberlech, Austria*
*Photo: James H Schriebl*

# BUILDING TECHNOLOGY

# Wet Over Dry

The year was 1991, and we had just launched our company. Our first commission was a gut renovation of an Upper East Side co-op studio apartment for a partner's sister. The apartment needed everything: electrical, air conditioning, floors, new windows, millwork, a new kitchen and bathroom—and just about everything else. As we do today, we sent our proposed plans, hand-drawn and hand-lettered at the time, to the building's managing agent, who in turn, forwarded them to the building's architect for review.

The building's reviewing architect was Elliott Glass, a fifty-six-year-old gentleman at the height of his power and fame. Power and fame may sound overstated, but not if you seek approvals to renovate apartments in the better buildings in Manhattan, especially the elegant Pre-War co-operatives that line Central Park West and Park and Fifth Avenues. I didn't realize when we received Elliott's review on that first project in 1991, we had commenced a professional relationship that would last my entire career. Now in his eighties, Elliott is still reviewing plans. Although he has no assistants and no succession plans of which I am aware, and although he represents fewer buildings than he did when he was younger, he remains the most highly regarded—and feared— building architect in NYC. If you think I embellish, please read an article written by Leslie Kaufman on October 24, 2008, in the *The New York Times*. The article is titled "This Man Could Ruin Your Renovation Plans," and if you were to ask most of my peers, the title tells the whole story.

Contemporary historians who study New York tell us that the 1970s was a low point in city history, especially from a residential real estate standpoint. The 1980s brought great recovery, but the economy crashed again in 1987. The 1990s kicked-off a thirty-year rise in residential values, and in spite of notable periodic retrenchments, residential real estate in Manhattan has been a good place to invest. As apartments became more and more expensive, co-op boards sought to tighten their oversight process on renovations. From his perch as the most respected reviewing architect, Elliott Glass established the standards by which renovations would be approved, and very often disapproved. Under Elliott's guidance, obtaining approval from a co-op board became more difficult than obtaining approval from the Department of Buildings. For those of us who came of age during the 1990s, we all agree that Elliott Glass literally wrote the rule book.

Following is a glossary of Elliot Glass rules/prohibitions that once did not exist, and are now nearly universal:

Wet-Over-Dry. These three little words are Elliott's most notable contribution to the field. We started hearing these three words in the mid-1990s, and twenty-five years later, a prohibition against wet-over-dry appears in almost every alteration agreement—the agreement between an apartment owner and the building's board of directors setting forth the terms under which an owner obtains approval for proposed renovations. Most apartment buildings are built in "lines", with each apartment being identical in layout to the one above or below. Bathrooms and kitchens are stacked, as are bedrooms, living rooms, libraries, dining rooms, etc. When we first started seeing in Elliott's review letters his objection to our enlarged bathrooms and kitchens, we assumed this was to prevent leaks from a bath or kitchen (wet areas) into a bedroom or living space (dry areas). This straightforward interpretation of wet-over-dry makes perfect sense, except that it doesn't.

The prohibition nagged at me. Installing proper waterproofing ensures that leaks won't percolate directly down, and since nothing prevents water from an overflowed tub from flowing out the bathroom door and over the saddle, it is more likely for an overflow to leak down to an adjacent living space on the floor below. While I was sure Elliott had his reasons for introducing the concept of wet-over-dry, I was missing a nuance. So I did what any presumptuous upstart would do, I picked up the phone and called him. I don't know if other architects call Elliott - not to debate or to argue, but to understand—but I have found the fearsome Elliott Glass to be open and candid with me every time I have made such a call. Elliott shared his thoughts as follows (paraphrased, as it has been many years since we had our conversation).

Elliot confirmed that I was right to question the notion that the wet-over-dry prohibition was primarily conceived to prevent water from traveling to the unit below. He shared with me his awareness that my professional colleagues and I were, as a group, presenting plan proposals to enlarge bathrooms and kitchens in response to requests from our ever-wealthier owners. It turns out we were also filling these larger bathrooms with whirlpool tubs (Jacuzzis), separate stall showers with large pan heads, and steam generators. The unintended consequence of the larger bathrooms with more plumbing fixtures was an increased load on the building's aged plumbing infrastructure, specifically the risers. While demolition operations expose risers within an apartment and provide an opportunity to address problems within the unit, Elliott observed that pipes were failing in other apartments on other floors, not just the ones being renovated. The failures were likely caused by a subject renovation, but since this could not be proven, the responsibility for repairs stayed with the building. The genius of Elliott's no-wet-over-dry language meant that the wet precincts could not be expanded to accommodate the increased plumbing that came along with the larger footprint and plumbing loads would not be increased. To make design solutions even more difficult, bathrooms needed to comply with adaptability standards of the ADA (American with Disabilities Act) as instituted by Local Law 58 of the 1987 NYC Building Code.

Today, much of the aged infrastructure in older buildings has been replaced and failures are less common than in the 1990s when Elliott first came up with the wet-over-dry prohibition. When seeking to enlarge baths and kitchens, we now share the above story with boards and often will get some relief, but not always, as too much precedent has been established and co-op board members are loathe to relax restrictions of which they had to comply when undertaking their own prior renovations.

Noisy-Over-Quiet. The next design prohibition that came into being was the rejection of noisy-over-qsuiet layouts, meaning we could not put a kitchen over a dining room. This is less frequently cited, and can often be mitigated by sound attenuation, but if Elliott Glass is reviewing your plans, you can expect meaningful resistance.

Garbage Disposals. Garbage disposals are NOT illegal in New York City, yet most building alteration agreements prohibit them. I made another call to Elliott on this one, and the hard to pronounce simple answer is arteriosclerosis. Once the garbage disposal has julienned the carrot, the pieces go right down the drain, out of sight and out of mind. Yet, as they descend and less water is flushing them to the basement, they begin to stick to the inner wall of the pipe. Most waste risers in apartment houses in Manhattan are four inches in diameter, yet I've seen old pipes that are occluded to only an inch of free area. This is probably a good time to beg our hygienic friends not to flush baby wipes or dental floss.

Pot-Fillers. I don't know if Elliott objects, but I always have. Imagine a young mom (or dad) filling a pot for pasta when her (or his) young child screams from the tub. Forgetting to turn off the water, the concerned parent rushes to the child's aid, forgetting the task at hand. How valuable is the art in the apartment below?

Whirlpool tubs. Have you ever heard a jet engine in a confined space? They also sound loud in the apartment next door, and in the one below, too.

Note 1.

I spoke to Elliott and told him I was writing this, and I thanked him for all his contributions in helping to establish best practices with regard to renovating apartments in New York City. He stands on the front lines telling people they can't have everything they want, but in every dealing I've had with the man, he has been fair, consistent, and advising for the greater good. No one likes regulations that hinder their ambition, but our city is a lot better off with Elliott Glass as a standard bearer.

Note 2.

In September of 2020, in the middle of the pandemic, I received the following email from Elliott. To say I was tickled would be an understatement; and at least for an hour or three during a very dark time, I was proud.

From: Elliott Glass
Subject: Writings
Date: September 6, 2020 at 1:17:26 PM EDT
To: Daniel Frisch

Dan,
I hope that you and yours are well and will continue to be, through and beyond, our present travails.
I could not wait for another day to pass as yesterday, while searching the web for an update regarding an old architecture classmate, I came across, for the first time, your Writings, and then, of course, the "Wet-Over Dry" writing of May 2, 2019 that I had not seen before. Be assured that I would have written you immediately if I had.

I must commend you for the article's thoroughness and, particularly, for its explanations of the reasons for many of the comments and judgments that I typically make. But, I am somewhat embarrassed by its flattery.

I am presently in the process of consolidating my files and moving to a smaller office in the same building. This process should be completed in the next 4-6 weeks. It would then be my pleasure to join you for lunch to catch-up on the world of architecture and other profound topics. Please keep in touch.

Warmest regards,
Elliott

# Indoor Plumbing - Manhattan Style

Manhattanites talk about plumbing the way New Englanders talk about the weather. Co-op boards and building superintendents bond over concerns about plumbing systems, when not endlessly discussing exterior waterproofing and city-mandated façade repairs. Most people understand that living in an apartment house represents a unique social lifestyle. Barking dogs, high heels, and bouncing balls all create noises that seem to amplify as they travel from apartment to apartment. Gossip travels even faster. And, nothing brings the social experiment into clearer focus than plumbing issues.

In 1882, the first city-wide steam system was brought on line in Manhattan. This shared infrastructure program presented a utopian vision of urban living; city dwellers would have clean, safe, and presumably cheap centrally distributed steam heat, similar to the gas supplied to homes throughout the boroughs for lights and cooking. A few decades later, gas lighting would be replaced by electric and the horseless carriage would replace the horse-drawn carriage, and yet, city steam would hang on through the 20th century and beyond. While many buildings produce steam or hot water for heating by their own boilers, Con Ed still provides steam to some 1700 commercial and residential buildings in Manhattan (according to Wikipedia). Studying the history of urban construction technology, the elevator's invention was the primary catalyst to erecting tall buildings. Plumbing technology, or lack thereof, was just as much of an impediment. When cast iron and brass pipes are stacked vertically, story after story, they create an unsupportable load distributed over a very small area. Over time, architects and engineers developed the practice of offsetting pipe risers every six or eight floors distributing the loads over a greater floor area, and skyward we traveled.

Residential architects in small firms in New York City rarely have the opportunity to design new buildings, but rather practice our art renovating and reimagining apartments and penthouses within buildings built many years ago. Irrespective of the age of the building, construction in New York City must comply with the NYC Building Code, which varies considerably from the national residential codes governing construction in other communities. This difference is particularly apparent in the rules and regulations concerning the licensed trades, i.e., electrical, HVAC, and plumbing. Throughout most of the country, electricians run their circuits in Romex, a flexible, plastic-shielded wire. The NYC electrical code, however, dictates the licensed electrical contractor run its circuits in "BX," a cumbersome aluminum shielded cable. Similarly, suburban plumbers exclusively use PVC pipe and pex tubing, whereas the NYC code calls for cast iron and copper. While these distinctions may seem technical or incidental, they are in no way trivial when it comes to material and labor costs. Other than the cost of business, the above has little impact on the individual homeowner. Few are interested or care what type of cable supplies their lighting or what type of pipe brings their water to their faucets, yet these distinctions matter a great deal to the architect and contractors specifying and installing the systems.

Three plumbing issues from New York City renovation projects illustrate what can go wrong. All three were discovered when leaks were reported by homeowners or aggrieved downstairs neighbors. The first two instances were the result of clogged waste lines and were not unusual. In one case the diagnostics (a camera sent down the pipe to determine the source of the obstruction) resulted in a he-said/he-said dispute as to the cause. Representatives of both parties were present when the line was scoped and snaked. The homeowner insisted nothing unusual had been flushed, while the plumber and contractor were equally insistent that baby wipes and paper towels were the cause. It is impossible for both statements to be true, and unfortunately, the dispute escalated when it came time to pay the bill. If Tom Wolfe were still alive, he would be able to write lines of dialogue perfectly describing the partisan perspectives of contractors and homeowners.

Since the clog was discovered quickly and addressed, the damage was minimal and limited to the homeowner's apartment. In this case, the downstairs neighbor did not have to weigh in with an opinion and a complaint – and another bill. With only minor inconvenience and with the expense of scoping and clearing the obstruction being just over 1,000 dollars, the matter should have concluded quickly—except this toilet had clogged previously. The owner was convinced, and maybe rightly so, that there was a flaw either in design or execution. Could the cast-iron waste pipe be poorly manufactured? Could the toilet have an inefficient flushing mechanism, an all-too-common problem due to water efficiency regulations? Which, for the record, we enthusiastically support. Could the plumber have installed the waste line with too little pitch? The homeowner believes the culprit is the design of the toilet, a wall-hung model with an in-wall tank. This is the least likely culprit. Wall-hung toilets, European style, so to speak have become ever more popular, and we expect them to soon outnumber conventional floor-mounted models. Most likely, today's 1.6 gpf (gallons per flush) toilets just don't have enough flushing capacity for the horizontal branch lines connecting toilets to the building risers of apartment buildings, and the contractor's advice to flush twice isn't such a bad idea. At risk of environmental blasphemy, maybe thee should flush thrice?

The second event was very similar except that the back-up was severe enough to flood the apartment and to leak into the apartment below, entirely changing the problem-solving dynamic. In addition to cleaning up the mess within the homeowner's apartment, the apartment below suffered damage. There is nothing unusual here, as there is only one way for water to flow. The building superintendent attended the diagnostics and snaking, and it was confirmed that the clog was at the end of the branch waste line, but before its discharge into the building riser (waste stack). This made the liability for repair, both the damage within the apartment and also within the apartment below, the responsibility of the homeowners and their contractor—and their respective insurance carriers. Once the cause of the incident is deduced and repairs undertaken, the question of how to prevent future incidents becomes paramount.

once again, my favorite recommendation came from the contractor to purchase an old-school toilet that would flush 3.0 gallons per flush—almost double the maximum gpf currently allowable. Using more water to flush a powder room toilet is more environmentally supportable, if not code compliant, than the frequent repairs caused by insufficient flushing power.

Our third story has nothing to do with clogged waste lines, but rather, an improperly installed shower pan. In our first two stories, we couldn't isolate a culprit other than the fundamental disconnect between modern living and aged infrastructure. In the case of the leaking shower pans, the villain was a contractor who failed to coordinate the plumbing and stone and tile teams. The NYC DOB code dictates that showers have lead pans installed beneath the shower floor. This lead membrane gets turned up the walls and the curb at the shower door. This 19thh century waterproofing solution gets water-tested, and in theory, provides a continuous inert pan to prevent leaks. In this example, the lead pan was installed and tested, but only formed a two- or three-inch-high pan. When the stone and tile crew came to install the shower floor, they filled the pan with concrete (properly sloped to the drain) and then installed the stone floor. Unfortunately, the stone floor finished at nearly the height of the pan. When the shower drained slowly and water pooled, the height of the ponding water was higher than the pan, and water overflowed, getting into the walls and eventually, traveled to the apartment below. Of course, this leak occurred well after the contractor had finished the project.

Electrical systems in large buildings present similar difficulties. Central air conditioning and electric ovens usually require increasing an apartment's electrical service. Once Con Ed and a building's board have approved the additional service, running new conduit or pulling new wires can be a daunting and expensive proposition. And the better the view, the more costly the upgrade, as such projects are priced by the distance from the service in the basement to the panel in the apartment. Even after a service upgrade has been performed, problems can persist. Most central air conditioning equipment requires 220-volt power, which is not available in all buildings. More discouraging still is little-known fact that certain equipment, including the most popular wall ovens, operate sub-optimally if voltage drops below 220 volts. Voltage drop occurs in

Manhattan, most notably during heat index days when Con Ed drops the voltage delivery in certain neighborhoods to 208 volts to reduce the risk of brownouts and blackouts. A few years ago, a client's dual-fuel range—electric oven, gas cooktop—had to be replaced with an all-gas model as the preheat time for the oven was running approximately forty-five minutes—not a happy circumstance for a young family thriving on chicken nuggets and French fries.

Having covered a little history and having told a few stories of unfortunate incidents, let's turn now to the future. Landmark Pre-War residential buildings line Central Park, not to mention Park and West End Avenues, Riverside Drive, much of the Upper East Side, and lower Fifth Avenue. Very early examples, such as the Dakota, date from the 19th century, and most of these Pre-War edifices were completed prior to the Great Depression. When originally built, apartments were large, but closets and baths were small and kitchens were the precinct of staff—not the beating heart of the home as they are today. While these shortcomings present challenges to designers when re-imagining homes for today's families, the greater impediment to successfully accommodating modern living is the aged infrastructure of our most picturesque and valuable residential buildings. Infrastructure challenges are now front and center of the minds of the co-op boards, building engineers, and architects entrusted with the stewardship of these civic treasures. Read the real estate section of the *New York Times* or glance through *Architectural Digest*, and it is to see just how expensive apartments are within these majestic buildings, which means the homeowners are wealthy—very wealthy—and also demanding. Within such expensive homes, central air conditioning is a must, as are electric ovens and gas cooktops, which may be replaced by induction. As more and more apartments are modernized and upgraded, and as buildings age, a conflict has arisen that we are just beginning to understand and to consider solutions. The gas lines (risers) serving individual apartments usually come into the basement, are metered there, and then run vertically to the individual apartments, often within the walls of other apartments on floors between the basement and the apartment. Each time a homeowner's architect files for new or relocated gas equipment (cooktop, clothes dryer, etc.), current Department of Buildings protocol is to test the risers for leaks, which may occur anywhere form the cellar to the apartment. If the pressure does not hold, which is proof of a leak, the gas is shut-off, only to be turned on once the riser is repaired or a new riser installed. Repairing risers buried within walls of neighbors' apartments is inconvenient if not impossible, leaving no choice for a building to either allow a new riser to be installed, or to tell the (very wealthy) shareholder, that there will be no "cooking with gas." And if not gas, well then, how about electric? Just show us where to run the new electric riser.

# The Luxury of Quiet

The week before the Fourth of July of 2023, I found myself speaking with Adriane Quinlan, a talented journalist from *Curbed/New York Magazine*, who was conducting research for an article on acoustics and codes in New York City apartment buildings. She had found occasions when neighbor-on-neighbor conflict due to acoustics had led to confrontation, from lawsuits to murder. She was curious as to how neighbor-disturbing inhabitant noise, everything from arguments, stiletto footfalls, piano practice, to electronic dance music, was covered in the building codes. Surely, she felt, the builders who build such thin and seemingly sound-amplifying walls between apartments must be in violation of some code. Adriane was also curious as to how compliance was enforced, other than dispute resolution by the NYPD. I am not sure I was much help to her, as we rarely design multi-family buildings and our details and construction specifications well exceed the bare minimum codes most developers follow. Notwithstanding, her questions got me to thinking about acoustic privacy between neighbors in our more familiar high-end market.

In the earliest days of cities, prior to electricity, indoor plumbing, and elevators, single family homes were typically rowhouses with shared wood-framed party walls, gas lighting, and outhouses in the rear yard. Subsequently, these rowhouses would be built with masonry party walls, yet still relied on heavy timber floor framing. Both types of homes can still be seen within the five boroughs of New York City, and throughout other cities of a similar age that have coherent zoning regulations and landmark preservation enthusiasts. The rowhouse still defines and dominates the urban residential landscape in many neighborhoods of many cities. As an example, our firm is overseeing the preservation and modernization of an original wood-framed house in Nantucket that is one of five conjoined rowhouses built in the 1830s. As we go through the archaeological process of demolition, we are transported to an earlier age, both in lifestyle and in construction technology. Notably, a neighbor let us know that he was worried by the early phase of exploratory demolition and by what may come after, as absolutely everything can be heard between the two houses. We will certainly specify additional insulation at the paper-thin walls shared with the home's neighbors.

Following the row houses were the walk-up tenements, essentially taller buildings constructed as double-wide and triple-wide townhouses of apartments with a common stair. Instead of serving one family or two, if one counts parents and staff, these tenements provided housing for as many families as could be accommodated and were in many ways the progenitor of slums. One can imagine that secrets among the tenancy were rare with so many living in such tight quarters. If only walls could talk, as the banging steam radiator pipes surely did.

This building typology featuring masonry walls and wood-framed floors could also be elegant, which I note every time I visit Venice, Italy, and see that this exact methodology was used to construct the palazzos that line the canals—without the fire escapes and overcrowding, at least within the grand apartments. In the States, and specifically in New York City, the Gilded Age brought us electricity, plumbing, elevators, and for larger structures, the two-way reinforced concrete slab. These construction technologies together allowed architects like Rosario Candela and Emery Roth to surround Central Park and grace the major avenues with their exuberant luxury apartment buildings we collectively refer to today as pre-war.

Enter one of these "Class A Fireproof" pre-war buildings and you can feel the hush, almost as if all sound has somehow been removed. Speaking in whispers seems the only appropriate behavior. This other-worldly nearly silent, old-world sensibility is the product not just of the doorman's demeanor and the intimidating countenance of the apartment dwellers, but even more so due to the construction technology beneath the confectionary ornamentation.

The grand buildings all feature rigid steel frames whose columns and beams are oversized by today's efficiency and economization standards, as their architects and engineers did not enjoy computer-aided design programs that enable the minimization of structure. The exterior walls are masonry—typically brick, limestone, or marble—and were built to withstand the test of time as they have. Inside the buildings, the floors are supported with thick, twelve inch two-way reinforced concrete slabs with an insulating layer of six to eight inches of cinder fill (vermiculite) above the slab and below the finish flooring. Sound transmission, whether vibration or air-borne, has trouble transferring vertically from apartment to apartment through this heavy mass of floor structure. Similar to the floors, the interior walls of these pre-war buildings were largely made from either terracotta masonry or gypsum blocks, bricks made from gypsum, the same material in today's sheetrock, which in turn, were covered in thick plaster. If you rap your knuckles on an interior partition of an older apartment, you will hear a deadness, with no drum-like amplification of a modern stud and sheetrock wall.

The post-war (WWII) boom brought a rush to build lighter, brighter, and less expensive apartment houses. Emery Roth, who gave us such wonderful icons as the San Remo and the Beresford, also brought us the post-war, white-brick superblock buildings of the Upper East Side, mostly as the successor firm Emery Roth and Sons. While the early post-war buildings shared many sensibilities and construction technologies with their pre-war brethren, gracious rooms and gypsum block partition walls, the developer-fueled rush to build faster and less expensively was on. Stud walls were invented, first heavy gauge steel with lath and plaster, and subsequently, light gauge and ever-thinner sheetrock – insulation optional. Gone, too, was the vermiculite fill as finish flooring could be more economically installed directly above the concrete slab, which was also getting thinner year by year. Neighbors could finally hear each other's whispers.

Today, when we renovate apartments in post-war buildings, one of the most important interventions we undertake is to improve sound attenuation between apartments. We routinely specify a floating floor system, with the wood floor installed over two layers of plywood subflooring laid perpendicular to each other, and with an acoustic underlayment beneath primarily made of especially reformulated rubber. We double the sheetrock and add sound batting between the wall studs. In extreme circumstances, the tracks in which the metal studs stand are installed over resilient channels and suspended sheetrock ceilings are hung on springs. When we are aware that neighbors are known to practice the piano, we build walls within the walls, seeking to create even greater sound isolation through separation and added mass. Having recognized the benefits of sound attenuation in post-war buildings, we also use many of the methods when working in the old-world, pre-war buildings. You simply cannot have enough sound separation between neighbors, especially for those who can afford to not hear one another.

While the foregoing assesses sound transmission and mitigation between neighbors in luxury apartment buildings, similarities appear when studying the construction of single-family homes in the suburbs and beyond. Walk through a significant older home on Long Island's North Shore or in Greenwich, CT, or in hundreds of other resort and bedroom communities, and you experience that same hush of the grand apartment buildings lining Central Park. These mansions—not McMansions—were built to last generations. The Frick and the Cooper Hewitt Museums on Manhattan's Upper East Side were originally single-family homes in the "country." The construction dissimilarities in mid-century suburbia are even more extreme than when comparing pre-war and post-war buildings in New York City. And yet, something interesting and maybe unexpected is happening. Today's energy, seismic, and hurricane codes are having an affirmative impact on single-family home construction, and in many cases, we are building better than previous generations. The codes governing the components of a home's exterior envelope (insulation, windows, sheathing) have all been strengthened, resulting in tighter buildings that save energy and are less likely to be blown away in a hurricane or reduced to rubble in an earthquake. By satisfying the energy, seismic and hurricane code requirements, properly designed and built new homes are more resilient, sustainable, and quieter.

And with electric cars making roadways quieter as well, homeowners will be able to open the windows and hear the birds trilling, provided the air quality allows letting in the outside air. Finally, the pandemic brought us a remote work culture, and when working from home, people are demanding greater sound insulation between rooms and between neighbors. Taken together, today's code-related and programmatic mandates are combining to create quieter homes, and optimistically, not just for those who live on Park Avenue or in an early 20th century mansion.

# Park Avenue Air Conditioning

This essay is a companion piece of sorts to the "Luxury of Quiet," although slanting a little more towards the technical. While the pre-war apartment buildings owe their quiet sensibility to the construction means and methods from when they were built, updated apartments often also benefit from more recently installed central air conditioning, a type of system that was not envisioned when these grand apartment buildings were constructed. Conversely, heat is usually still delivered as it was when the buildings were built, through a low-tech and antiquated system of steam risers and radiators. In most cases, this heat pours forth at much greater volume than necessary due to the early 20th century need for residents to leave their windows open in winter to flood apartments with pandemic-combatting fresh air. As for yet-to-be-invented air conditioning, early residents relied on open windows, fans, and cool drinks—and the option of relocating to mountain estates in the Adirondacks, or to the seaside resorts of Newport, the Jersey Shore, and the Hamptons, and closer to home, to hamlets like Locust Valley and Oyster Bay. (Long Island's North and South Shore towns which were the models for F. Scott Fitzgerald's East Egg and West Egg.)

Creating heat, from a physics standpoint, is straightforward (fuel + fire + water = steam). Air conditioning, however, is more difficult, as almost all systems run on electricity, and a good amount of it. In 1902, Willis Carrier invented and installed the first commercial air-conditioning system at the Sackett-Wilhelms Lithographing and Publishing Company in Brooklyn to cool and dehumidify the factory, and to keep the reams of paper from curling. The system was displayed to the public at the 1904 World's Fair in St. Louis. The auditorium and other rooms of the Missouri State Building were cooled through mechanical refrigeration; at the very same World's Fair, also known as the Louisiana Purchase Exposition, the ice cream cone was invented. By the 1970s, most commercial buildings incorporated whole building air-conditioning systems and multi-unit residential buildings followed suit. Single family residential applications were much less common until the 1950s when window air conditioners became an attainable commodity for affluent homeowners. Where large commercial buildings relied on whole building solutions—typically chillers on the roof and air-handlers and ducted distribution systems throughout the building—most residential buildings sought post-construction solutions by which individual units would have individual control of their air-conditions, and ideally on a room-by-room basis, just like rural and suburban homes. The solution was the same, install individual room window air conditioners, and occasionally, through-the-wall versions (usually below a window).

The great "white brick" buildings in Manhattan of the forties, fifties, and sixties introduced PTACs (Package Terminal Air Conditioners) which merged heating and air conditioning systems for individual rooms in large buildings. The through-wall units sit under street or court facing windows and have both a room air conditioner and a connection to the building's hydronic or steam risers for heat. For those not so familiar with large apartment buildings, these PTAC units most resemble the combo heat and AC units in a Motel 6, and not surprisingly, are substandard technology for luxury apartments in the most expensive zip codes in the country. And yet, when we oversee gut renovations within these white brick buildings, we replace the existing PTACs with exactly the same type of units with their mid-last-century technology.

For renovations within pre-war buildings, we have real central air options. Together with our engineers, we design systems with through-wall condensers underneath courtyard windows, connected by line sets (piping) to air handlers within the apartments, that are in turn ducted to the rooms. While this may sound complicated, the system is more efficient and stable than PTACs or individual through-wall air conditioners. We only need to cut one hole in a building exterior to handle approximately 1500 square feet of interior space. Straightforward, yes—easy, no.

We have overseen the installation of central air conditioning within individual apartments in the pre-war creations of Rosario Candelo, Emery Roth, Delano & Aldrich, and Van Wart & Wein, and modernizing these grand apartments is a fun challenge. The process starts with design and engineering and once plans are prepared, they are submitted to the building's managing agent, who sends them along to the building's architect and engineer for review, comment, and after multiple rounds of revisions, eventual approval. Once approved by the building's team, the plans are sent through to the NYC Landmarks Preservation Commission and to the Department of Buildings for their respective approvals. Many architects and engineers will contend that getting approvals is more difficult than designing and installing the systems. I feel differently. While easier with repetition, the design and installation is still daunting.

Before contemplating the installation of central air, the building's electrical service and delivery route needs to be assessed and compared with the electrical power requirements of the new system(s). The electrical service to an individual apartment will frequently need to be upgraded. We were recently tasked with designing renovations to an estate condition apartment in the tower of one of Emory Roth's most famous edifices fronting Central Park. Fortunately, we knew the building's reviewing architects and engineers, and had the opportunity to collaboratively brainstorm the routing of an additional electrical riser running the twenty-one stories between the basement and the apartment. The new riser had to run horizontally along the basement ceiling from the electric meter room to a fire stair, and then vertically for the twenty-one stories in the space between the handrails of the turn-back stairs. It is quite likely that our apartment owner will be the last one afforded space in the fire stair to run a new riser, the space is now packed solid.

So, why do we do it? I would love to answer by simply saying we love the challenge, but while this may be true, the answer is simpler. The benefits of central air well outweigh the difficulties and expense. As we replace leaky windows with modern insulated windows to save energy and to keep out exhaust fumes and soot, modulating the interior climate has taken on even greater importance. Today's systems can control both temperature and humidity, and can also purify the air, removing pathogens while creating a more comfortable environment. Central air systems are quieter and more energy efficient than their through-wall, through-window, and PTAC brethren. And if an owner ever wants to sell an apartment post-renovation, central air is probably the number one amenity from a return-on-investment standpoint. Winner, winner, chicken dinner.

# Cars, Cooktops and the Net-Zero House;
# The Great Electrification

**Electric cars.** I grew up in the Michigan rust belt of the 70s and 80s, and it seemed all that Motor City across the state could muster was unrefined and unrestrained muscle. Without broadcasting to my friends, and certainly not to their Michigan-proud parents, I pined for the European offerings, and even in a pinch, what Japan was exporting. It's no wonder my first car was a barely running 1965 Volkswagen Beetle, nor that my next car as a collegiate was a 1975 Saab with over 120,000 miles when purchased with the earnings from a hard summer's labor. As an adult, I have become an evangelical advocate of summer jobs for high school and college students. The "Wagon Duck", as we affectionately called my Saab's unusually designed hatchback, was a perfect fit despite its many design and mechanical quirks for a preppy and elitist future architect. Even with three mechanics seemingly on call in Charlottesville, Virginia, the car broke down frequently and absurdly inconveniently, and finally, sadly, my parent-sponsors insisted she be traded in for an example of dependable American sheet metal. In 1997, I reestablished my relationship with the now defunct Saab Motor Company. I brought home my first-ever new car, a black 9-3 Convertible to a Manhattan garage with a monthly rent nearly as dear as my apartment. It was the first of four black Saab convertibles I leased in secession, the last being the 2007 Aero convertible that we now own and is wintering in our garage—and appreciating as the years tick by. She won't be sold, though; and we count down the years to 2032, when the kids can gleefully hang antique car plates on her. I realize in writing this, the first one I leased in 1997 would already be eligible, and soon enough, our 2012 Subaru and 2013 Jeep Wrangler will qualify, as well.

Architects form deep connections with their cars, and I am no exception. The cars I've known and loved all have been gasoline-powered, at least until Elon and Tesla came along, upending the world with every new offering. On a pleasant Saturday in March of 2022, without much on the agenda, I walked the kids west from Lincoln Center to the Polestar showroom, which Polestar calls a "space." I hadn't told them of the spreadsheet I had created comparing range, price, and zero to sixty times of several available electric vehicles. Quietly, my wife Darcy and I had spent months weighing the pros and cons of electric vehicles and finally decided the time was right to consider signing on. We were aware the cars we favored were more expensive than gas alternatives, that we wouldn't likely enjoy a road trip in an EV other than a Tesla with their dominant supercharging network, and that repairs or service, if necessary, would be expensive and inconvenient. We also failed to contemplate what would happen in the case of an accident (foreshadowing). An hour after our visit to the "space" and a very quick test drive, our family of four went out to lunch and hotly debated colors and option packages. Well-fed, and in surprising agreement, we wandered back to the "space" and were guided through placing a deposit online. Buying or leasing an EV from one of the electric-only manufacturers is a new and discomfiting experience for us not-so-young people who thrive on relationships. There is no manager with whom to cajole and negotiate, there is no car to drive off the floor, and there are no customers loitering in the showroom looking to kibbitz and compare notes while waiting for the service department to complete their oil change, as EV's have no oil to change.

Six frustrating months after the originally promised lead time of six weeks, we finally took delivery of our first electric vehicle. The handoff occurred not at the "space", but in Chelsea at Manhattan Motor Cars. Surrounded by a fleet of exotic six figure performance cars, both electric and internal combustion, the delivery process took a little more than an hour and was led by an upbeat twenty-something techie and an even younger trainee. Finally checked out on this unfamiliar machine, I drove away, an iPad-like tablet staring at me as I did my best to keep my eyes on the road. We aren't particularly early adopters when it comes to EV's, some ten percent of all new cars sold in 2022 were electric, and yet, as we became familiar with the car, we experienced the opposite of buyer's remorse. Our thoughts were akin to "what took us so long." The car is superior in so many ways to any car we've owned. It is quieter. It is faster. Its handling is truer. The adaptive driving—not yet autonomous—and safety features impress and will likely compel even more as we adapt to the technology as over-the-air updates float down from the cloud to magically update the software at the heart of the vehicle. Best of all, the car's first scheduled maintenance comes at 30,000 miles or three years, and we no longer need to stop for gas when driving back and forth between Connecticut and New York. Together, these affirmative attributes overcame our knowledge that electricity is produced neither cleanly nor efficiently, and that plans are murky for the recycling of batteries. We even overcame the fact that our Swedish performance car was manufactured in China. But, following the old expression, a better mousetrap is just that, a better mousetrap.

When the public agrees that electric vehicles are better than gas alternatives, market forces will accelerate the transition, not by regulation and mandate, but by demand. Brought about by the need to reverse climate change, EVs represent the future, both for the planet and for drivers and passengers. Someday in the not-too-distant future, renewable energy will prevail, improved capacity batteries will be more easily recyclable, and our self-driving cars will pilot themselves to roadside charging sites that are as ubiquitous as the gas stations of the 20th century. I can't help but be reminded of the famous introductory lines of Star Wars: "This story happened a long time ago in a galaxy far, far away. It is already over. Nothing can be done to change it."

Note: As for the aforementioned accident, our love affair with the car only lasted a sum total of 1432 miles before striking a deer (an eight-pointer by estimation) at fifty miles per hour. Luckily no one was injured—except the deer—but the car sustained significant damage. Under normal circumstances, the car would have been put on a flat bed and towed to a certified autobody shop and repaired. In this case, Polestar had not yet certified any repair shops, nor could the company provide a parts list, cost, or lead time for the supply of OEM (original equipment manufacturer) parts, and our insurer had to total her out. Unlike the long wait for the first car, the replacement car we are now driving was in stock and ready for delivery.

**Gas Cooktops.** The appliance world hits a little closer to home and not just because I love to cook or that among my most treasured possessions are my mother's cast iron pans that have been perfectly seasoned by nearly a century of blue flames. As the specifier of appliances for clients' homes, we are constantly learning which appliances are loved and most desired. Built-in steam ovens, high BTU wok burners, and sous vide vacuum drawers are the current rage, with luxury appliance manufacturers racing to dominate each respective category. We also hear the myriad complaints when appliances reliably underperform or fail. By example, I learned last year that the very best clear-ice maker has a life expectancy of only seven years. We also take note of once-popular products that have gone out of fashion: trash compactors, for instance. Lately, we've been hearing drumbeats of potential regulations targeting the nearly universal gas stove. Maybe the gas stove is the next incandescent lightbulb. I, however, struggle to imagine reconsidering my preference for gas stovetops. From the clicking of the igniter to the visual management and constant adjustment of the blue flame, cooking with gas is a sensual experience. And yet, we are now hearing from thinktanks and our government's suggestions that gas stoves present a health risk, especially in poorly ventilated kitchens. The headlines are curious, given the modest health risks of gas stoves—which are by no means assault rifles or cigarettes after all—could be addressed by encouraging better ventilation or by an education campaign about ventilation and gas stoves—a little fine print, if you will. The health risks, therefore, are likely the proverbial tail wagging a Saint Bernard, adding fossil fuel to an already blazing fire.

New York City is seeking to address climate change in 2023 by prohibiting gas service to new buildings under seven stories, and in 2027, this regulation will expand to include all new buildings. For the past decade, failed gas inspections within existing structures, whether routine, or a result of 311 complaints—"I smell gas"—or necessitated by projects filed with the Department of Buildings, have made restoring gas service difficult to the point of near-impossibility. Residents commonly recount that they and their neighbors had to cook on hot plates for a year or more while Con Ed inspected and oversaw the replacement of leaking gas lines. The city and the Department of Buildings clearly have gas service in their gun sights, even before adding in the notion of health risks. While both city and national governments are keen to facilitate the transition from fossil fuels to clean electricity, the transition will not come easily and won't be contested solely by a cook's nostalgic preference for the blue flame. The changeover of cooking, not to mention heating plants and clothes drying, from gas to electricity is either a Herculean or Sisyphean task, depending on your level of mythological cynicism.

Using New York City as an example, there are roughly 77,000 residential buildings with four or more apartments throughout the boroughs of New York City. Add in the one-, two-, and three-unit townhouses, there are more than one million existing residential units, and for the some 400,000 (forty percent) that have gas stoves, converting to electric will be difficult, expensive, and take decades or longer. In larger buildings, finding space in the mechanical areas of the basement for additional larger electrical meter pans presents logistical challenges, and once power is brought to the building and space is made available, running conduits vertically, story after story, to individual units is even more daunting. For an apartment on the twentieth floor of one of the landmark Emory Roth towers along Central Park West that required an electric upgrade to power the central air system and electric wall ovens, we were graciously allocated space in the cellar meter closet. From there, conduits were run along hallway ceilings for approximately 150 feet to a fire stair, and then up we went, and up, and up, and up—some 250 feet up. The electricians followed a route taken by others, utilizing the limited space between the handrails of the switchback fire stair, filling the vertical void effectively solid. As we discussed with the building's chief engineer, we were lucky to find the route, and it is unlikely the next wealthy homeowner in need of an electrical service upgrade will be able to find a similar route. Perhaps, the New York Landmarks Preservation Commission will greenlight the running of conduits on the exterior of one of the most notable buildings in Manhattan. I'm not holding my breath.

Other problems with power persist in our largest city. Con Edison cannot deliver enough power to the borough of Manhattan on the summer's high demand days. On these heat index days, Con Edison dials back the power delivery to Manhattan residents to avoid brownouts and blackouts, the blackout of 2003 being the most extreme example in my memory. For residents in certain neighborhoods, power can be decreased for most of a summer. It is even worse for residents who live on high floors and suffer additional voltage-drop as the electrical conduits climb to the sky. It can take unacceptably long to preheat a large bespoke electric oven to cook a child's chicken nuggets. For a penthouse project, sixteen floors in the air, we had to have Wolf Range replace the dual-fuel range with an all-gas model due to this problem—ironically, the exact reverse of today's desired conversion of gas to electric. Come visit me in the office, and you will see a stunning Iwan Baan photograph of a dark lower Manhattan that graced the cover of New York Magazine just after 2012's Super Storm Sandy. The sobering image documents what happens when a significant portion of the grid supplying a city of eight million souls fails.

In New York City, these challenges and more will require market forces to combine with safety and climate concerns to make gas stoves a thing of the past, just as gas lighting and gas ovens are no longer the standard of the day. The preference for electric ovens did not come about due to the very real early 20th century health risk—death—of sticking one's head in an oven. That vexing problem was solved in the 1960s by changing the chemical make-up of gas delivery. Electric lighting was originally thought to be less safe than the gas lighting it was replacing—it wasn't. The change to electric lighting and ovens is purely functional, which is obvious with lighting, but less so for ovens. Today's electric oven holds temperature more precisely, is readily programmable, and most importantly to the homeowner, is self-cleaning. Today's space-efficient digitally programmable electric air-fryers preheat almost immediately, fry without oil, use less energy than traditional larger ovens, and can be purchased at Amazon and plugged into standard outlets.

As for the offending, blue-flamed cooktop which has grabbed recent headlines, a straight-up comparison to an electric induction unit may help. With induction, pasta water boils faster, burners simmer at a lower and more precise temperature, and when the saucepan is not in contact with the cooktop surface, the surface is cool to the touch, effectively "child safe," even though children predictably prove there is no such thing. And just like the electric oven, an induction cooktop made of flat glass is much easier to clean. For high-heat wok cooking, the top-of-the-line induction burner provides 30,000 equivalent BTUs, compared to the best-in-class gas burner at 22,000 BTUs—and the induction wok's pointed bottom magically hovers a few millimeters above the glass surface. Given time, even the most nostalgic and egotistical chef will demand to make the switch to induction. The only question remains is whether I will be as excited to cook in my mother's pans. They are ferrous, so they work with induction, but somehow I fear the experiential disconnect between technologies separated by a century may be too much for me.

**The Net-Zero House.** Moving on from cars and cooktops, we come to the net-zero house, a subject about which residential architects have greater expertise. If you are a rancher with exceptional acreage, and are a wildcatter to boot, we can probably design for you a net-zero house that hums along on site-harvested fossil fuels. For everyone else, the dream of being off-the-grid and consuming no more energy than produced on premises requires an electric-only energy solution, both in production and consumption. Today's technology makes the ideal of a net-zero house realizable, no longer just the futurist imaginings presented at a World's Fair or at GreenBuild, the US Green Building Council's annual convention. Renewable energy sources are all available at the residential scale, and the electric systems become more efficient with each passing year. While each of our new home designs is energy efficient, satisfying or surpassing codes and qualifying for energy management certification (LEED, etc.), we have yet to design a fully net-zero home. We have installed solar and geothermal systems, and we have even designed all-electric homes, and while not yet net-zero, the future is coming.

Most homeowners carefully consider the cost-benefit assessments comparing the up-front expenses to the savings in operating expense. While variable, the time it takes to recoup the up-front capital investment through operating savings has historically been intolerably long and is made all the greater by the significant incremental cost of designing and installing aesthetically pleasing systems. Forgive me the political statement, but fossil fuels, even with the rise in costs at the pump, are still too cheap.

Even more than the prolonged return on investment of renewables, net-zero houses are often unattractive, covered in flat plate solar collectors, and maybe with a wind turbine out back. Most people do not aspire to live in an industrial designer's vision of a machine for living. But as we get better at it, we specify aesthetically non-compromising solutions such as building integrated solar. (This includes thin film adhesive collectors installed between the standing seams of a metal roof, geothermal that is buried under ground, and solar thermal with pex tubing run below dark roofs heated by the sun and which pre-heat domestic hot water and radiant heat storage tanks.) When we finally resolve the cost-benefit and aesthetic considerations, net-zero homes will become more desirable and less rare. In the meantime, we'll continue in our grid-tied ways – just don't ask us to let you cook with gas, unless you really want to.

---

Every day, the transition from fossil fuels to renewably generated electricity becomes more certain, and while the impetus may have been climate change, the accelerant is demand. On February 14, 2023 the New York Post published an article titled: "See Blade's futuristic new 'helicopters that will bring NYC's elite to the Hamptons – quietly;" about Blade Air Mobility's test of its new eVTOL (electric Vertical Take-Off and Landing) aircraft. Just as with electric cars, electric vertical aircraft (EVA) will be zero-emissions. More significantly, EVAs will reduce, or remove altogether, the intolerable air pollution of helicopters—a tremendous relief for those who live or work in Manhattan and the Hamptons, some of the country's most expensive zip codes. I imagine it will be some time before I hitch a ride on an EVA, but we should all be thrilled that billionaires have created a market for engineers to solve their rare-air problems. Those of us who are less fortunate and more than a little jealous—and who hate rotor noise as much as they do—will be even greater per-capita beneficiaries of its disappearance. At the end of the 19th century, the exceedingly affluent were the first to install electric lighting in their homes, and at the end of the twentieth, were the first to hang flat screen (plasma) TVs on their walls.

# House of Tomorrow

The first time I shared this essay, it was sarcastically titled "The Not-So-Smart Home." I was immeasurably frustrated with home integration strategies and had become convinced that the promise of a truly "smart home" was unattainable, and the effort to make technology behave was more troublesome than beneficial. From a building technology perspective, labor-saving strategies have changed the way we live. Imagine the 1898 Paris World's Fair (Fourth Exposition Universelle) that brought together Bell's telephone, Edison's light bulb, Otis' elevator, and gave Eiffel's tower to Paris and the world. The "House of Tomorrow" refers to George Fred Keck's glass and steel house installed at the Second Chicago World's Fair in 1933. The home featured central air conditioning, the first dishwasher by General Electric, an "iceless" refrigerator, and an automatic garage door operator. Just a few years later and closer to home in Queens, New York, the 1939 World's Fair theme was "Building the World of Tomorrow" including a competition to design the "Home of the Future." Most notable was opening day at the RCA pavilion with its first public demonstration of the television – a live broadcast of a speech by Franklin Delano Roosevelt.

Baby boomers fondly recall *The Jetsons* and their otherworldly romanticization of the automated home. While the 1960s appliance ads of the *Mad Men* era look quaint, albeit in a most misogynistic manner, they document the enthusiasm for labor savings attained through technological innovation. Coming of age as an architect in the digital

90s when technology integration and the smart home were no longer the province of science fiction made for fits and starts. The highs and lows began for us when the first plasma screen televisions arrived, at a minimum system cost of $20,000 apiece. Once the television was affixed to the wall and was no longer concealed in millwork or an antique armoire, we sought ways to hide the equipment. Centralizing AV systems was challenging for both television and music. For large apartments and homes that called for audio and television in many rooms, we installed columns of cable boxes, amplifiers, power conditioners, and music sources in custom-made racks in dedicated closets with fans whirring 24/7 to keep the equipment cool. For whole-house music, we progressed in a few years from 500 compact disc shufflers to designated and expensive digital servers, all to accomplish what an iPhone and Sonos do today with elegance and simplicity. Speakers were all hardwired and often permanently installed in-wall. Along with the AV wiring came the need for programmed universal remotes. Nothing frustrated homeowners more than a basket of remotes with Post-It Notes describing which buttons on which remotes needed to be pressed in which order. Couldn't there be just one remote to control music and television? The answer was always "that is just a programming issue." Every time there was a glitch, however, the programmer had to come out to the home to assess and to reprogram. Predictably, the consultant would attribute the glitch on a faulty piece of equipment or worse, would blame the owner for pressing the wrong buttons too impatiently. Once this had occurred a few times, the homeowner usually became frustrated at the bugs and started to look for simpler workarounds. Sometimes we replaced the consultant—although this was difficult due to the proprietary codes—and as a result, programming-intensive pieces of equipment became abandoned and the baskets of remotes with their Post-It Notes reappeared.

The digital age brought many opportunities. We could control the lights and shades, and the heating and air-conditioning systems too. Watching a living room transform itself at the touch of a button to a Hollywood quality screening room is very compelling. Unfortunately, these integrated systems often failed to work smoothly and were challenging to service. The final nail in the coffin for me came when we would visit friends and clients in their homes, and upon taking note of all the expensive yet non-functioning technology, we began to refer to them dismissively as "technology museums." In an effort to help friends and clients not repeat the sins of the past, we started to humorously refer to ourselves as "dis-integration advisors."

And now, I can mark the precise day that I changed my mind. The day was June 24, 2021, and we had spent the morning with clients in appliance showrooms learning about steam ovens, ice makers, and an induction wok. As for the wok, you "have to see it to believe it." The pan doesn't make contact with the cooktop surface, yet still inducts to an otherworldly 31,000 equivalent BTUs, twice the output of a conventional high-output gas burner.

Our last appointment was with Lutron for a demonstration of their new Ketra lighting system. Similar to audio-visual centralization, we have been working for years to transition from conventional lighting solutions to LED. When we first started utilizing LEDs (light emitting diodes), we had two primary paths. The first was to install new LED bulbs in conventional line voltage fixtures, and the second was to specify and install new LED fixtures with their "chips on board." From roughly 2010 to 2015, we thought the bulb replacement approach was preferential as we could purchase and install new bulbs as offerings improved. Neither approach worked well during the frontier days of LEDs. Color and hues were inconsistent, lights flickered and strobed, dimming was problematic, and when all else succeeded, fixtures and dimmers buzzed. Some of these challenges were easy to solve, others persisted and until the June 2021 presentation, I was convinced that whole-house lighting control was as problematic as centralized AV.

What I saw in the Lutron showroom made me as excited as the Paris Exposition visitor must have felt at seeing Edison's lights or of hearing Bell's voice, or when beholding the Eiffel Tower. As the lighting changed from day to night and back again, it was as if I were enjoying a light installation by James Turrell. I was overcome by optimism that lighting design could finally fulfill the promise of LED, and not just in a Sky Space, but in one's home. On display, were lights that could dance. They could change color endlessly and dim to one percent (not forty). They didn't strobe, flicker, or buzz. These groundbreaking fixtures are also more "tunable" than others and the lights can be set to any color of the spectrum—red, orange, yellow, green, blue, indigo, violet—and any color temperature from sunset to daylight. Better still, each fixture is "addressable,"'meaning they are controlled wirelessly and individually. This approach will reduce the number of individual wire runs for lighting by roughly eighty percent or more, and will allow the decision of how to group lights to occur post-occupancy, as opposed to during the design and construction phases. While the fixtures themselves are expensive, some of the cost will be offset by the simplicity and efficiency of their wiring. As for the programming of these new fixtures, there will not be proprietary codes locked away in the audio-visual consultant's safe, but they will be programmed remotely by using the Lutron app, a laptop computer, and a smart phone. I don't believe many homeowners will undertake this task, but at least they won't be at the mercy of a single consultant.

As for the house of tomorrow, Lutron and its new product Ketra have truly helped me to see the light, and just a little more than usual, I find myself inspired and "Looking Forward."

# Wood Windows

Like all passions, my passion for residential architecture is deeply personal. I grew up in a mid-century modern house with a flat roof—in western Michigan, of all places—with three smokestack style chimneys, a split-level entry, and a forty-five-degree orientation on its meager partial acre lot. The house was stained charcoal grey—black—with white trim and a fire engine red front door. Never has there been a house better designed to receive and display thereafter airborne eggs on Devil's Night (Halloween eve). The house featured a near curtain wall of south-facing aluminum windows and sliding glass doors, and given its orientation, was an early example of a passive-solar home, before passive solar design was popular. This extremely remarkable house in an otherwise unremarkable Grand Rapids suburb had a tremendous influence on my youthful fascination and love for architecture.

During high school, I spent a summer in Cambridge, MA, as a student in the Harvard University Graduate School of Design's (GSD) Career Discovery program. The GSD is housed in Gund Hall, a modernist wedge-shaped building designed by Australian architect and GSD graduate Jon Andrews (1972). To get from the studios to Harvard Square, we usually walked through Harvard Yard, home to some of the country's oldest structures. The difference in architectural idiom was lost on none of us. Many of the buildings on the Yard date to the 17th century, and at the photographer's golden hour, their original leaded glass windows shimmer magically.

At UVA, we got to know the Lawn and the Rotunda, Jeffersonian architecture writ large; we often visited and studied Monticello, arguably the first architect-designed American residence. Next time you have occasion to visit, take special note of Jefferson's triple-hung windows and the chain-driven simultaneously closing French doors. These meticulously preserved examples of 200-year-old wood windows and doors are exceptional. Soon after college, I remember visiting friends in Siasconsett on Nantucket. The family home was at the very eastern tip of the island—as far easterly as you can be and still be in the United States—and the 200-year-old wood ocean-facing windows were subjected to extreme salt and wind conditions. That summer, the sashes were brought down to the yard and we repainted them (aubergine if I remember correctly). Perhaps with appropriate maintenance and stewardship, they will last another 200 years.

Graduate school brought me to Columbia University, a New York City campus designed by McKim Mead and White, with countless wood windows to study, even while enrolled in a school dominated by deconstructionism. Post-graduation, I joined the profession, and have since had the opportunity to work on and restore numerous landmarked properties in New York City and beyond. We've been fortunate to document and preserve and/or replicate windows dating back 250 years.

The earliest versions of double-hung sashes traveled up and down in vertical wood channels. To keep a sash in its open position, one could either insert a peg in a hole in the jamb or place a block of wood on the sill. Both options are low-tech and very effective. The simplicity of the design and the few moving parts of early wood windows ensured their durability.

The engineers of the next generation of double-hung windows sought a solution to keep windows in any open position. Ingeniously, designers fashioned counterweights with chains and pulleys hidden within a vertical chaise at the side of the sashes. The concealed counterweights weigh the same as the sash and the sash balances in any position. The system also delivered the benefit of making the sash feel weightless when opening. My family once rented a Riverside Drive apartment in a landmarked co-op built in 1907. Within the apartment were three of the original oversized weight-and chain windows. After more than a century, these three windows operated more effortlessly than any of the modern aluminum replacement windows throughout the rest of the apartment, which were no more than twenty years old.

Properly maintained historic wood windows can last indefinitely. I've often used this experience and the above anecdotes to assertively lobby clients to install wood windows and sign up for the perpetual maintenance associated with painted wood windows. Further study – continuing education of a sort - has made me rethink this recommendation.

Modern manufactured wood windows are superbly engineered. Air infiltration is reduced to almost nothing. The sashes accommodate double and even triple glazing. Sound infiltration can be addressed, and UV transmittance can be reduced. Conveniently, sashes can be tilted in for cleaning.

Manufactured modern wood windows, however, differ materially from their ancestors in both material and engineering. To save costs, manufacturers have switched from old-growth dense hardwoods to lighter pine species. To reduce the variability of working with a natural product, sashes and frames are machine planed and finger-jointed, creating a precise product that can satisfy rigorous laboratory testing and can be warrantied by the manufacturer. Unfortunately, modern production techniques cannot make soft wood hard. Problematically, pine also has a lot of sap and resin, making the material less ideal for painting or staining.

The second challenge facing the perpetuity of today's wood window is its modern mechanism for raising and lowering the sash, and most importantly, for keeping the sash at its intended position. Whereas first-generation windows ran up and down in simple channels and were held in place by pegs, and second-generation windows were of the weight-and-chain variety, modern windows run up and down on something called sash liners. These are concealed and inaccessible tracks, usually made of plastic. Instead of chains and counterbalances, the windows are held in position by leaf springs, which fatigue over time.

While I've been telling my stories and recommending painted wood windows for years, I feel we've gotten a bit lucky in that clients have often opted for a more cost-effective option: windows clad in aluminum or fabricated entirely out of composite materials. For die-hard preservation cases when budgets are expansive, we can still specify custom-fabricated, historically accurate windows, either weight and chain, or reproductions of pegged colonial era windows—both of which can last generations; but for the rest, we've moved on.

With both humility and wisdom, I realize my nostalgic bias for historic windows has been tempered by a life of continuing education.

# Brand Ambassadors

When I first started visiting jobs as a professional, I became fascinated with the similarities from project to project and contractor to contractor. Most notably, they all used the same power tools, not just the same manner of tools, but identical brands. It seemed every drill was made by Makita, as were reciprocating saws ("sawzalls"), unless they were by Milwaukee—which were also the two brands dominating the palm sander market. What wasn't prevalent was a Makita or Milwaukee circular saw or jig saw—I am not sure I have ever seen one. On job sites, circular saws were by Porter Cable or DeWalt, and jigsaws were always Bosch—no others. The only decision the professional carpenter seemed to make was whether to use the Bosch D-handle version or the barrel-handle version. I observed that brands were so consistent that it was unimaginable for a company like Ryobi - which makes a great hand router—to break into one of the sub-markets for a specific tool. Does anyone other than Dremel even make a multitool? Apparently, the two great competitive equalizers of price and advertising have little impact when a professional is purchasing a tool. Even today, with Lowes and Home Depot and crowd-sourced reviews, a few specific brands dominate when we conduct our field inspections.

This observation about tools and brands has a perfect corollary in the world of appliances. Most major appliance manufacturers make appliances in every category, yet we rarely specify the same brand for more than a couple of appliances in a home. Wolf dominates ranges, and

Sub Zero is dominant in refrigeration. Wolf doesn't make a refrigerator and Sub Zero doesn't make a range, although they are now owned by the same parent company. Miele is the go-to for dishwashing, with Bosch running a distant second. Scotsman is a leader in icemakers; they even make units for Sub-Zero. Today, Samsung, Electrolux, and LG are all battling for position one in the clothes washing and drying market. Other brands pop up now and again, but the market share leaders in each category are well known and consistent.

I've speculated that carpenters and tradesmen know something about tool selection and that there may be a similar basis for consistent and repetitive appliance selections. Recently, I learned at least part of the answer. When we built our house (2014-2015), we, like any other consumer, went to our local appliance store and picked appliances. The owner of the store was quite insistent that I purchase the market preferred Miele dishwasher. We followed his lead and installed two in our kitchen. I don't love them as much as we had hoped. The plastic soap dispenser broke on one, and unlike the old Maytag commercials which portrayed a napping repairman (Maytags are just that reliable...), I had the opportunity to meet a real live Miele repairman.

Replacing a broken soap dispenser is a straightforward proposition. Remove the outer door, a stainless door liner, and insulation; pop out the broken dispenser, install the replacement part, and reassemble. This operation took the mechanic all of fifteen minutes, even with me sitting on a stool asking questions. The mechanic was young, I am guessing twenty-five or so, but he impressed me as confident and knowledgeable. As we chatted, I learned that he was a second-generation appliance repairman, that his dad owns the firm, and that he had been going out on service calls since he was little. I told him that our mutual friend and colleague, the owner of the appliance store, had insisted I buy the Miele machines, and that I continue to be unimpressed. To my surprise, the young mechanic told me he agreed with the sales pitch and set about demonstrating.

He went to his truck and brought back an oversized Lenovo laptop that he placed on the counter immediately above the dishwasher. Next, he plugged in a small wire to the laptop and with a suction cup, attached it to the top of the door where the program readout is on the machine. After a few moments, the dishwasher and laptop were communicating with one another, and the technician could now adjust the factory program settings on our machine to optimize performance. It turns out that every Miele dishwasher has this capability, and according to the technician, none of the competitors do. He also extolled the soundproofing of the units, stating that the Miele machines are approximately fifty pounds heavier than comparable Bosch machines. Et voilà, there really is something to Miele's place atop the dishwasher heap.

Lest you think this is a paid advertisement for Miele, the mechanic also said that we should stay away from Miele refrigerators, one of the few appliances not manufactured directly by Miele. The industry favored Sub Zero is the way to go. With only anecdotal data, I feel we can validate our practice of specifying by observation and popularity, it's no different than buying a saw.

# Material Substitutions -
# Learning from our Mistakes

With our shared passion for design, residential architects and homeowners spend countless hours researching, comparing, and specifying a home's materials. Sometimes, we nostalgically pine for materials of a former era, and other times we push forward into uncharted waters in a quest for the new, unique, or innovative. When we are not relying on the tried and true, we scour the shelter magazines and tirelessly tour stores and showrooms in search of perfect products. Selecting and specifying materials for a home is at its heart an optimistic and affirmative process. If successful, the home will be beautiful and stand the test of time. Whether we reference Steinbeck's *Of Mice and Men* (1937)—first penned by poet Robert Burns—"The best laid plans…," or attribute events to the Law of Murphy, things unfortunately do not always perform as advertised. While the years have taught us to bring a questioning ear to a great showroom pitch and to raise our eyebrows while captivated by architectural "porn," our enthusiasm in our quest for the new, new thing remains undiminished. Notwithstanding, we haven't always made it through the selection and specification phase unscathed and sharing what we've learned seems a worthy endeavor. Some of the stories in this essay date from the early days of our practice, and others have occurred recently. Perhaps, these illustrations will prevent one or more new stories from being written.

The Volatile Organic Compound Act of 1987 (VOC) came into existence four years before the 1991 founding of our firm, and in those early days, architects and contractors were only slightly aware of the impact the law would have on construction methodologies. For several years, oil-based paints and polyurethane floor finishes still enjoyed market dominance. Manufacturers upped production in advance of the law, and being very shelf-stable, pre-1987 grandfathered product remained widely available. Almost imperceptibly and without much fanfare, manufacturers began to dilute their oil-based offerings to comply with the VOC law. Product performance suffered and with no other choice, manufacturers invested in improving latex and water-borne formulations. It would take a dozen years for the industry to fully switch from oil-based to water-based products, and I can remember the project that demanded our firm toe the line as well. The year was 2002, and we had just completed a project on the Upper East Side of Manhattan and soon after our client moved in, we noticed the crisp off-white crown moldings were yellowing. We asked our product representative from Benjamin Moore to visit the apartment to assess. None too casually, he admitted that Benjamin Moore's then-recent oil-based formulations were having trouble remaining color-fast and the company would provide us the latest and greatest latex paint to replace—and $3,000 of labor as well, if I would solemnly swear not to specify their oil-based product again. regardless of which old-timer painter demanded we do so. For these next twenty-plus years, we've honored the deal.

Stone and tile choices fill a second warehouse of memories. If asked when younger to name my favorite color, I would most likely have answered "gray: it's neither black nor white, and I live in between." This fit my sense of humor and is similar to the engineer's aphorism that the glass is neither half-full, nor half-empty; but twice as large as it need be. My peers and I obsessed over gray building materials. Gray dominated as a choice for kitchens and bathrooms, and even for walls. It seemed that almost all Manhattan properties listed for sale were painted pewter gray - thank you, Calvin Klein (and John Pawson, the brand's British designer). The favorite bathroom stone was Batik Azul, a gray limestone that perfectly matched this minimalist gray sensibility. As with all limestone, Batik Azul has a soft appearance and is very porous. When marketed to us by the showrooms and vendors, we were assured that modern impregnating sealers would ensure that the stone would maintain its appearance for years. Repeated dousing with shampoos and conditioners prove that sealers fail, and the beautiful Batik Azul showers turned splotchy white. Try explaining to a client that the stone hasn't failed, it's just the sealer. The reason doesn't much matter when the only solution is to rip out the material and start anew. While today's quartz composite and porcelain materials do not look quite as soft as Batik Azul, we can now satisfy our less frequent gray urges with less fear of returning to the job after a short period to redo a home's bathrooms.

We also favored a veinless gray kitchen counter marketed as Basaltina. Basalt (the generic name for Basaltina) is very hard, evenly dark gray in color, and seemingly well suited for kitchen counters. Like Batik Azul, however, Basalt is porous and reliant on sealers to perform well as a kitchen counter. Soon after we completed our first kitchen featuring Basaltina counters, dark stains appeared and the family with young children reported that the only food prep they had performed was unboxing pizza. The grease had bled through the cardboard and penetrated the counters. The second and last time a client picked Basaltina, we were brought to the apartment to inspect the tell-tale dark stains. Sure enough, the stains were from similar cooking oils. Luckily, or so I thought, the apartment was located just across Fifth Avenue from Eataly, and I jogged across the street, bought a bottle of extra virgin olive oil and tried to stain the counters evenly. This did not work and we had little recourse but to convince the vendor and fabricator to replace the counters at the vendor's expense with a composite quartz material.

Moving up the radio dial from the 1990s to the aughts, we come to glass tiles. Throughout that decade, it seemed every high-end tile showroom's walls were covered with seductively shimmering back-painted glass tiles in aqueous hues of blue and green. We learned phrases like "back-butter thickness" and "crack suppression membrane," both of which implied specific instructions for properly installing glass tiles to prevent cracking. Some jobs went smoothly, but others developed cracking issues. We learned to order extra tiles and to keep a stock on hand as replacements. Invariably, we were told by our vendors that the problems stemmed from contractor unfamiliarity, if not incompetence. Sometimes, the room's underlying construction was to blame. I recall one project that had an adjacent elevator which was blamed for vibrating the tiled wall. Most frustratingly, a consistent undertone emerged that our cracking tiles were a problem unique to us, and that other specifiers and installers were not experiencing the same failures. At another project we were so concerned that the mechanics might not follow the supplier's strict and explicit recommendations that we color-printed and laminated forty pages of instructions and tacked them to the wall like wallpaper so the installers could not miss them. The tiles still cracked. Fortunately, the trend has largely passed, and we are left holding our breath on fewer projects. Sometimes it is better to learn to favor a different aesthetic rather than keeping endless boxes of replacement tiles in the storeroom.

Today, one of the more popular trends is encaustic tiles—cement tiles with pigment throughout the tiles, as opposed to a glaze on top. Various forms of encaustic tiles date from the middle-ages; many can still be seen in churches, cathedrals, and palaces throughout Europe. Today's versions are usually vibrant and modern in their patterns and are frequently featured in the shelter magazines. We have used various manufacturers' tiles with mixed success—better on walls than floors where shower products pool and pond. In a project completed during the pandemic, the floor tiles effloresced, and a chalky residue appeared on the surface of the tiles. Not only did this not go away, water and soaps defeated the impregnating sealer leaving behind dark stains at the floor. After two or three attempts to clean and reseal, we had to finally recommend to the owner that the tiles be replaced. After a bit of research, we found a porcelain tile line that is nearly indistinguishable from the encaustics they strive to emulate. In this case, we'll have a very reasonable material substitution to offer to the next client who falls in love with a picture in a magazine.

My final story under the heading of "Material Substitutions – Learning from our Mistakes" has to do with PVC decking. The marketing materials on PVC and composite decking tell a wonderful story of maintenance-free decking with twenty-five to fifty-year life spans, as well as cradle-to-grave environmental benefits as the boards are largely recycled and no rain forests are threatened. Dig through the marketing materials and you can find no downside to these synthetic materials - other than the cost. For a recent project, the PVC decking we specified was more expensive than the mahogany alternative. The dark boards we installed, however, warped in the sun's heat and after a few months, the effect could only be described as "oceanic." We hopped on a conference call with the project's general contractor and project manager, the local supplier, and two representatives from the manufacturer. Despite the company's marketing collateral including the tag line "everything wood should be" the material does not perform effectively as rooftop decking. During the first hour of the call, the manufacturer's representatives steadfastly asserted that the material had behaved as expected, even if inconsistently with their marketing materials. The representatives contended that the entirety of the fault lay with the installers, who had failed to understand the nature of the product. During the second hour, the ocean tides turned and the conversation became productive with a collaboration of ideas for improving the rigidity of the substrate, decreasing the board lengths, and changing to a lighter color. When the call finished, the manufacturer offered to provide all the materials necessary to stiffen the framing and replace the decking at no charge. We look forward to specifying mahogany going forward.

Reaching the conclusion of this essay, I don't regret one square foot of the Batik Azul or Basaltina we installed, nor the glass and encaustic tiles that required replacement, nor even the PVC decking. Designing and building homes is an exciting balance between the expected and actual, and there is no better route to education and future accomplishment than participating in both successes and failures. All we ask is that our clients stay patient while we treat their projects as our laboratory and find elegant solutions to problems as they arise.

# Annual Maintenance is a Tough Sell

Like the proverbial cobbler who has holes in his soles, I could do better heeding my own advice. The most recent indication can be summed up in one word: "filters." In my case, the term applies to both water and air conditioning filters. Seven or so years after our house was finished, our water pressure had diminished, slowing to a near trickle, and our air conditioning was struggling to keep up with a heat wave. The water pressure problem was solved when technicians discovered the whole-house water filter needed changing, and that it had needed replacement for some time. The struggling AC system was similarly fixed by a mechanic cleaning the dirty filters. If I were looking for a free pass, I could assert that others should have taken care of servicing the systems and cleaning and changing filters at our house, but saying so would be disingenuous. The responsibility to stay on top of these things is mine, and I blew it.

Since architects solely provide design services and don't manufacture, fabricate, or build, we don't have a product to guarantee. Even so, we enjoy ongoing, often lifelong, relationships with many of our clients, and treat these relationships as if we had offered a lifetime warranty. Even if we haven't kept in close touch, we are often the first call when something goes wrong. Sometimes a request is as simple as checking our records for a paint color for touch-ups; other times more extensive repairs are required due to mechanical failure or a leak. Instead of feeling imposed upon, we see visiting with former clients in their homes as an opportunity to say hello, reminisce, and assist. All too frequently, these visits also bring to light that our clients haven't followed our advice regarding annual maintenance any better than I have. There are many reasons for this.

Even when we most strongly advocate for clients to budget for annual maintenance, it often gets overlooked. There never seems to be a good time to regrout tile or refinish wood floors, nor are contractors easy to find and schedule. In many cases, the contractors who originally built the residence have become fully engaged with new work and coming back to a previous project is an inconvenience. Additionally, contractors are invariably hesitant to appropriately charge for a call back, even years after the work has been completed and the warranties have expired. A charge, even one which is not great enough to cover the contractor's cost, feels like a nuisance fee, and the interval between project completion and repairs rarely feels long enough for the homeowner to feel the contractor shouldn't be accountable. Contractors appreciate the sentiment and to protect their relationship with their former clients either put off or ignore the request, or more likely try to accommodate the request, treating the work more as a favor than legitimate business. More homeowner-contractor relationships have deteriorated in this manner, when it would have been simpler for the contractor to schedule the work, to perform the work consistent with the original project, and to send an appropriate invoice.

Having witnessed the above scenario countless times, we have come to understand that general contractors and maintenance companies are two profoundly different organizations. General contractors excel at scheduling and executing full projects from start to finish, managing and coordinating teams of subcontractors and vendors. Maintenance companies arrive at an occupied home to perform discreet repairs. Rarely have we found a single organization that excels at both types of work. While this observation clarifies the difficulty, it doesn't pose much in the way of a solution to the challenge of essential ongoing maintenance and we have yet to find a one-size-fits all answer.

With much encouragement, we have found some general contractors are better at performing maintenance work for former clients. Some recognize the value of nurturing these relationships and have integrated maintenance work into their organization. When we do recommend a general contractor come back years after project completion to perform out-of-warranty repairs and maintenance, we always recommend they charge for the work and that clients pay with a smile. This is the best although somewhat rare outcome.

For other clients, we need other solutions. The first and most essential is to have clients set up service contracts with certain trades to perform regularly scheduled maintenance—just like we all do for our cars and for our teeth. Cleaning and changing filters can be a calendar event, and a service company will even send out reminders. Try getting a general contractor to do that!

Service contracts will keep you cool and your water pure, but fail to address other needs like refinishing floors, paint touch-ups, stone sealing, and fixing things that break. A number of companies in Manhattan and Brooklyn have been formed to provide jack-of-all-trades repairs for homeowners. Unfortunately, we've found the best of the breed to be prohibitively expensive, and lesser companies are under-resourced or poor matches for our client's homes and quality expectations.

In the meantime, we nag our clients and friends to have us over for a glass of wine—otherwise known as an inspection—and prepare an annual scope of repairs, which we will then help them source. In the best cases, our general contractor partners join us in the endeavor. To date, I can think of only three friends/clients that have taken us up on this year-in and year-out. They have all been very successful in business and life. I like to think their approach to home and other endeavors are related.

# AT THE OFFICE

# Go Piss in Your Boots

"Go piss in your boots" sounds like a colloquial insult, a rebuke delivered with a clenched jaw. For nearly 40 years, that's exactly what I thought it was and yet, an internet search turns up little. Similar expressions do exist, with "To pour piss out of a boot'" as a reference to stupidity being my favorite.

I don't recall how Coach Adam Streitel found his way from Germany to Grand Rapids, Michigan—did I ever ask?—but in the late seventies and early eighties, he brought his great passion and love for football (soccer) to a group of impressionable provincial teenagers. We believed he had played goalie for the German National Team around the time of the Korean War, but none of us really knew the details. We never asked. Nonetheless, we hung on his every word, even when those words frustrated us. Frequently, practices found us never touching a ball. He stressed conditioning, one of many coaching strategies that were ahead of his (or our) time. But still, a whole practice without scrimmaging?

We all liked winning, and together we put up a very favorable won-loss record. And when we did touch the ball, we learnt that a potent offense starts with a formidable defense, the ball is quicker than the player, and that frequent passing is much more effective than one person dribbling up the field.

Coach Streitel also tried to extend his authority beyond the pitch. Whenever my parents attended a game or picked me up from practice, he would implore them to feed me steak. I was undersized and if I were to be competitive, I would need to be bigger and tougher. To this day, I hold Coach Streitel's limited nutritional expertise responsible my love of flank steak—especially the way my father prepared it: on the Weber with Worcestershire and garlic salt.

Coach Streitel was also a psychologist. At the end of one particularly exhausting practice, I complained to Coach that my new cleats had given me blisters. Without missing a beat, he said that if I peed in my shoes, I would not thereafter get blisters. I was startled and opted not to urinate in my new and very dear shoes. Needless to say, it was the last time I complained to Coach. Problem solved.

One evening, we were playing a tight match and adrenaline was running high. Blister-free, I found myself running the midfield close by our team's bench and bleachers. At the far end of the pitch, the opposing forward broke through our defense, generating a one-on-one with our goalkeeper. The forward rifled a perfect shot toward the upper-right corner of the goal, a near-certain score. Our keeper leapt, then seemed to pause in midair. At the last moment, his arms shot out. As he came down with the ball, our bench and fans let loose. At this, Coach Streitel turned his back on the field and faced the bleachers. "Shut up," he told the cheering fans. "That is his job."

All these years later, when one of our team does something truly exceptional, Coach Adam Streitel's words replay in my mind. Fortunately, the phrase stops there, before it can leave my mouth.

Reflecting on my training with Coach Streitel, I understand why competitive athletes often succeed in high-stakes careers, most notably in finance positions with objective win-lose accounting metrics. An exceptional coach can instill the habits, skills, and single-minded ambition that cutthroat fields reward. But how might those lessons apply to a collaborative process where encouragement is as necessary as iron-fisted direction? Creativity requires lateral thinking. Often, the most brilliant solutions to a problem come from people who aren't afraid to admit their misgivings about a given proposal or pause when everyone around them is pushing forward. At DFA, our scale usually tilts towards affirmation. What motivates on the ball field comes up short when we are faced with complex challenges that require elasticity and nuance.

Balance is the key. Some of my most vivid memories are of goals scored and others narrowly missed, and, perhaps even more so, of the camaraderie of those never-ending practices. The many lessons I learned through competitive sports, especially team sports, have set me up well in life. To this day, I abhor participation awards and am convinced that honest, uninflated report cards are an important and valuable tool. The balance I seek comes not from lowering expectations or tolerating poor performance but rather from inspiring excellence through sports-like discipline within a steadfastly nurturing environment.

Like Coach Streitel, I realize that leadership means wearing many hats—though I personally refrain from offering nutritional or psychological guidance. And although I sometimes worry that Coach would be appalled by the affirmative support we provide at DFA, it is through no lack of appreciation for his wisdom that I have yet to tell a complainer to go piss in their boots.

# We Keep Our Own Report Cards

As our firm has grown and matured, we've established a set of core principles. One of these is "We keep our own report cards."

Clients and contractors provide us near-constant feedback, both celebratory and critical. The feedback helps us hone our craft and improves the quality of our professional services. Yet, heartfelt communication can also mislead. The process of designing and building homes is intimate, emotionally charged, and without fail, disconcertingly expensive. Assessments are often emotionally biased and can reflect competing agendas. Client and contractor wishes are often oppositional and impossible to simultaneously satisfy. While we welcome glowing reviews and expressions of appreciation from clients, as well as their criticism, we sometimes find this feedback constructive, and at other times less so. For our young associates in particular, negative comments can be devastating and praise equally dangerous. I decided we needed a more objective system to accurately evaluate our performance.

The Owner-Architect and Owner-Contractor Agreement Forms published by the American Institute of Architects (AIA) set forth that the architect is to be the neutral arbiter between owner and contractor. This concept is a core building block of the architectural profession. To fulfill this Solomon-like mediation role, we've learned to both listen and to tune out. When a client or contractor encourages us to take a side, I often remind my colleagues that the firm has been hired to respond in the best interest of the project.

Taking this neutrality as our standard, we have designed a project report card form that we fill out at the conclusion of each project. We meet as a team to answer a handful of questions. These include big-picture assessments: How did the project turn out? Was the client pleased? We also pose more nuanced questions: How did contractors, consultants, and our team perform? How was the budget managed, both during design and during construction? What particular obstacles were overcome? Did the project incur delays, and could they have been avoided?

This firm-wide debriefing process establishes and reinforces our culture of self-assessment and objectivity. What have we done well? How have we struggled? How can we do better?

# I'm Not Good at Math

*Four people stand on one shore of a river and are keen to get to the opposite shore as quickly as possible. The "rules" stipulate that an individual can cross the bridge either alone or with a companion. As it is dusk, a flashlight must accompany each crossing. Each individual walks or runs at a different rate and can travel the bridge respectively in one minute, two minutes, five minutes, or ten minutes. When traveling as a pair, the two individuals travel at the slower rate. For example, if the one-minute traveler goes with the ten minute, it takes ten minutes to cross and one minute to return with the flashlight.*

*Q.: How can all four travelers get to the opposite shore following these rules in seventeen minutes?*

Half a lifetime ago, a cousin shared the above riddle with me. He claimed the problem was one with which Microsoft executives tested potential hires. I struggled mightily at first to solve it and for a short time I was indignantly convinced it was impossible and that the riddle was flawed (the answer is at the end of the essay). More recently, the same cousin shared another favorite interview question – "Why are manhole covers round?" – which I have borrowed and use to this day to see how candidates react to a question when they do not know the answer and cannot simply Google it. In 2012, William Poundstone published a non-fiction book titled, *Are You Smart Enough to Work at Google?: Questions, Zen-like Riddles, Insanely Difficult Puzzles, and Other Devious Interviewing Techniques You Need to Know to Get a Job Anywhere in the New Economy* (2012). Having read much of this book, I would be no more likely to get a job at Google,

Microsoft, or anywhere in the new economy. Fortunately, I sit on the other side of the table these days.

Interviewing at our firm is less intimidating than applying for a job at Microsoft or Google, even if we often ask candidates why manhole covers are round (the answer is also in the footnotes of this essay). We do seek to understand how potential hires solve problems, especially under pressure. We also try to tease from candidates their career goals, which can be awkward for candidates seeking their first job after years of study. While few candidates arrive in our conference room with a well-defined five-year plan, quick thinking and finding solutions to life's immediate and long-term riddles are part of our every day and all interview topics are fair game as a means of communicating this. We have never gone so far as having given a challenging math riddle, as the math problems we solve are generally straightforward and math fluency is something we take for granted of future architects who possess at least one professional degree.

We use math every day, most of which is simple algebra and geometry, and never as much as quadratic equations or the derivatives we studied in calculus. Our student conviction that calculus, a prerequisite in architecture school, has little real-world use in the design and architecture fields has been confirmed. We use math to perform simple tasks like calculating area (square footage) and evaluating budgets, often on a price-per-square-foot basis. We undertake these tasks conversationally and, in most cases, without the help of the calculators or computers on which we rely when precision trumps estimation. When calculating square footage, anyone in our office (except myself) can place a cursor on a to-scale plan, and working around the perimeter of a room, apartment, or building, have the computer provide a precise square footage calculation. When a scaled plan is not available, a computer is not of so much use, and square footage approximations are extrapolated by adding up individual rooms. Sometimes we pace off spaces. From many years walking golf courses, I can get eerily close to building dimensions by knowing how to walk with an exactly three-foot gait (yards to the hole in golf). Sometimes we count tiles and multiply. Sometimes we look at the proportion of a wall to judge a ceiling height. While we do use tape measures, laser measuring devices, and now LiDAR scanners, it is amazing how often the tape measures and lasers are not at hand—and our LiDAR downloads will not arrive for a week.

When interviewing interns, and then when training them for a career in architecture, we rarely pause to think that the basic math we use daily might intimidate. And yet, we all too often hear a response to a very basic mathematic question of "I'm not good at math." The reflexive reaction "I'm not good at math" comes without even hearing the question. While I try not to be overly reactive, I don't always handle this situation well. I want to blurt, and sometimes do, "this isn't calculus, this is multiplication…" I know I should have thought twice before printing and laminating the multiplication tables for a young associate who was particularly struggling. As might be expected, the associate soon found another job with a nicer boss.

Turning more serious, "I'm not good at math" is a symptomatic of a reliance on technology, no different than resolving arguments by asking "Alexa" or by using ChatPT to write an essay—this essay was written and rewritten—without such assistance. I suppose I take after my mother, whose favorite subject was math and always said, "math is fun: math is just a game." I wish more people felt this way, and I sure hope my kids do.

*Answers on next page.*

*Bridge Riddle Answer:*  *The one and the two go over (two minutes spent), and the one comes back with the flashlight (one more minute expended for a running total of three minutes). Next, the five and ten go over together (ten more minutes for a total of thirteen), and the two runs back (fifteen minutes expended). Finally, the one and two go over again for a total of seventeen minutes. Once solved it seems so obvious, no?*

*Manhole Covers Answer:*  *Why are manhole covers round?  We have heard creative responses including the ability to roll them from place to place, to using less material (saves money), to being less likely to cut one's foot on a sharp edge. The real answer is that a round manhole cover cannot fall thorough on a person below, no matter which way the cover is turned. This, too, comes down to math, specifically geometry, and understanding the impact of the hypotenuse of anything other than a circle. A combination of Vitruvius and Newton in one simple question.*

# Why Are Manhole Covers Round?

Come visit us on Fifty-Sixth Street and you will find hanging behind my desk a colorful full-size deeply embossed, monoprint of a NYC manhole cover. It proclaims the word SEWER, in reverse, on thick handmade paper. Printed in the street in 1992, by an artist-team with whom I am friendly, this work continues to rank as one of my favorites in our collection. Not only do I admire the image and the ingenuity of its creation, but it has also become a mute accomplice when interviewing potential employees. Many have heard the urban legends surrounding Microsoft and Google math riddles designed to keep interviewees on their toes and to help decide which of the Mensa candidates should be hired.

For our interviews, I borrowed a question from a cousin who runs a private company here in Manhattan: "Why are manhole covers round?" Most recent graduates coming to interview have not heard the question and become off-balance, maybe not as much as "tell us about your five-year plan," though perhaps they should be. Imagine being twenty-something, sitting in an office with a middle-aged architect and a couple of associates at a firm where you would like to secure a job offer and being asked why manhole covers are round. On the surface, the question is simple and seems like something a prospect with a degree from a top-tier architecture school might be expected to know—and yet, most don't.

When a candidate doesn't know the answer, he or she must make a series of quick decisions, including trying to figure out the question's context. Why has this question been asked, instead of something about my portfolio, academic accomplishments, or career goals? Very often, the first response is to ask if the question could be repeated. Next comes the guessing game. The two most frequent guesses are that round covers can be rolled from place a to b, or that a round manhole cover would save material over a square. Both are true, but neither is the real reason. Only once in a great while can a candidate figure on the spot, even with prompting, that the reason is to save lives; round manhole covers cannot fall through the hole no matter which way they are oriented.

Provided the candidate has not read this essay or otherwise knows the answer, nor is one of the few who quickly stumbles upon the answer, our conversation becomes very informative. Going through the first couple of guesses goes quickly, and we can talk about how one solves a problem when the answer is "I don't know." Most candidates are very uncomfortable admitting a lack of knowledge, as I am certain I would be if the roles were reversed. What we like to see is a candidate who engages in a conversation filled with questions and follow-up questions. A robust back and forth is better than fielding ever further afield guesses or responding to an offer to Google it.

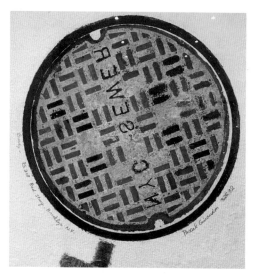

*Pascal Giraudon/Steven Lowy,* Respect (Bedford- Stuyvesant,
Brooklyn),
*1992, Mixed media on paper.*

# Game Theory

I love playing games, which means what it should and is not simply a euphemism for being manipulative. I grew up playing board and card games, everything from checkers, chess, Mastermind, to gin, pinochle, and even the Japanese game of Go. By far, my favorite games were word games like Jotto, Boggle and Scrabble. When playing Jotto, a game in which opponents try to guess each other's hidden words, I'd play without paper, mentally picturing the letter combinations and possibilities. For a number of years, I was the reigning family Boggle champion, which is frequently recounted at holiday get togethers. Today, both at home and office, we all play the daily *New York Times* "Spelling Bee," a game whose goal is to make as many words as possible from a flower-looking diagram featuring six letters surrounding a central letter. Each of us tries to score enough points by finding words, especially the one or more pangrams which incorporate each of the seven letters, and to achieve "Genius" status. On not so rare occasions, working individually or together, we succeed at finding every possible word and a cute bee icon appears on our phone indicating that we are "Queen Bee" for a day. It is a fair observation that I gravitate to people who like to play games.

One of the many lucky breaks from childhood was having parents and a specific aunt who nurtured my game-playing passions. My scientist father and I usually battled over the chess or Go boards, both being strategy games where the of luck of the draw or a roll of the dice cannot influence an outcome. In theory and practice, the better more experienced and more focused player most always claims victory, and

I suffered many defeats. My Aunt Alyce, on the other hand, favored backgammon and card games. She even had decks of cards imprinted with "Make Checks Payable to Alyce Lesser." I never asked what games she played for money, likely it was gin or bridge or both, but it was clear to me that games were to be taken seriously, and score was to be kept.

I brought a backgammon board with me to college and often played with dormitory friends, the same way my mother played bridge with her classmates a generation before. I vividly recall playing backgammon during my first semester at school with a particular hallmate, probably for a dime a point. We played many evenings and invariably I would win, a few dollars here, a few dollars there. When it came time to settle, I was ahead by a few hundred dollars, which was an extraordinary and inappropriate sum for first-year college students in 1983. This was no reason to rejoice, as my opponent was a defensive end on our college football team—something I might have considered before deciding to play him for money.

Regardless of the stakes, playing games for money elevates intensity and increases player adrenaline. Las Vegas casinos host backgammon and poker tournaments and to some, this condemns them as disagreeable games of chance, and those who play are denounced as back-room gamblers. Their attire and behavior on national television would not suggest otherwise. In spite of the mathematics at the heart of backgammon and poker, the games are taught and contested in dimly lit rooms, not celebrated in afterschool programs. Joining the school's chess club, on the other hand, is lauded; no differently than making the math team or signing up for science club. Chess club is rightly grouped among STEM extracurriculars and winning a state-wide high school chess tournament will certainly burnish a college application, much more so than cashing in an internet poker tournament and winning a seat at the World Series of Poker in Sin City.

Everyone should learn to play chess. As the proverb states, "Life is a game of chess," and two-plus centuries ago, Benjamin Franklin elaborated, "The game of chess is not merely an idle amusement. Several very valuable qualities of the mind, useful in the course of human life, are to be acquired or strengthened by it... Life is a kind of Chess, in which we have often points to gain, and competitors or adversaries to contend with." You will find no argument from me, except that the rules and complexities of the game wholly exclude the element of chance. For this reason, I prefer backgammon and poker, whose dice and cards introduce chance, and are a better simulation of the game of life. Poker and backgammon both trade on odds, and with each card dealt and each dice roll, the probability of winning is adjusted. Additionally, poker has its "tells," and the concept that if you can't recognize the sucker at the table, it may just be you. Kenny Rogers' most famous song "The Gambler" implores "that you need to know when to hold 'em; know when to fold 'em." It would be very challenging to know how to do this without constantly processing and reprocessing the statistical probabilities (the odds), not to mention having the ability to recognize whether an opponent is bluffing. The card and checker play, math, observation, and risk management skills needed to win at poker and backgammon correlate with life beyond the baize and board. And for record-keeping purposes, I may be the first and probably last person to favorably compare Kenny Rogers to Ben Franklin - which makes me smile.

Enjoying mountains of bad press, it is easy to understand poker's bad reputation, but it is a little less clear for backgammon. While people do play for money, I hardly think dear Aunt Alyce would have enthusiastically taught me a morally suspect pastime, any more than she would have encouraged me to drink or smoke, although she enjoyed both. Backgammon is a noble game played by small groups in every corner of the globe, and I am proud to be teaching my young children to play. Most decisions in backgammon come down to mathematics, whether it is the odds of being hit and sent to the bar or assessing who is ahead in a running race. Risk-reward is always top of mind, and while the play may seem straightforward, more subtle issues of timing can baffle. In other games, would players describe high double rolls as "too fast?" The most intriguing and unique element of backgammon is the doubling cube, a device that has no bearing on the playing of the game, but everything to do with its strategy. The six sides of the doubling cube are marked with the numerals 2, 4, 8, 16, 32, and 64 and the cube is not employed until a player offers it to his or her opponent. When a player feels he is ahead, before he rolls, he can offer to his opponent to double the point value or the stakes of the game by turning the cube to "2". If the opponent feels the game is a likely loser, he can decline the double, thereby conceding the game. If, on the other hand, the opponent feels he has a reasonable chance of prevailing, he can accept the double and take possession of the cube. Should the circumstances reverse and the player who owns the cube now believe the table has turned, he can offer the cube back at double the value, turning the cube to "4". As the game continues the same concession/acceptance process is repeated. When games are at their most exciting, the cube is passed back and forth a number of times, exerting exponential leverage and a near-constant need for reflection and reassessment. To make matters even more interesting, a simple win is tabulated based on the value of the cube, but if a player fails to bear off any checkers, the game is considered a "gammon" and the value is doubled. If a player has checkers remaining in his home board, the game is termed a "backgammon" and the game is trebled. Fortunes can change with a roll of the dice, and then change back again just as easily, and yet no matter the rolls, the better and more experienced player usually wins (sound familiar?), but the element of chance contributes unpredictability, excitement, and most importantly, hope!

While backgammon may be my favorite game, I'll play anything. If I could find a group with whom I enjoy playing late night poker, I'd be all-in. Buoyed by nostalgia, I've recently refinished a modern chess set designed by Lanier Graham in 1967 and purchased at MoMA by my parents when new. On a number of occasions, I've tried my hand at bridge, perhaps the most challenging of games. Bridge requires not only math skills but also fluency in a private language. Learning the game later in life is akin to picking up a foreign tongue without living abroad. Having difficulty understanding the bidding and table chatter is frustrating for me, especially since it is known that the best and the brightest play bridge, as evidenced by my mother-in-law who attained the status of Life Master. And yet, in spite of my curiosity, access, and ego, my kids are probably spot on when they tell me, "No Chance."

For now, I'll stick with backgammon and an occasional poker game, and maybe seek out a boutique manufacturer to print up a few decks of cards which read "Make Checks Payable to Daniel Frisch Architecture."

Note:  This essay was written in 2020 before "Wordle" caught the nation's imagination. I allocate more hours to the game offerings of the *New York Times* than all other social, entertainment, or educational online explorations. I know I am not alone.

# Bill James Baseball Abstract

Anyone who has sat through our Monday morning meetings would expect this segment to be titled "Money Ball" after Michael Lewis' 2003 book titled the same. My memory is often jogged by a rebroadcast of the 2011 movie starring Brad Pitt and Jonah Hill, and I frequently reference *Moneyball* (W.W. Norton, 2023) and that team victories stem from position play. My father introduced me to the subject while I was in high school. He not only coached my tee ball and Little League teams, he also helped found the first Rotisserie Baseball group in our hometown. From spring training through October, a bunch of academic and out-of-shape middle-aged men would meet weekly, check on their players' performance, compare notes, trade players, and compute the standings of their teams. Stats were looked up in the local paper and in *The Sporting News*. Al Gore had yet to invent the internet, and records were kept by hand on graph paper or ledgers, before the era of spreadsheets.

On my bookshelf, after all these years, remains a lone copy of a paperback volume titled *The Bill James Baseball Abstract, 1984 Edition*. The tag lines on the cover are from *Esquire Magazine* and read: "A Must for Fanatics," and "It's a Whole New Ballgame!" Inside the covers is a trove of statistics from the 1983 season on every team and player in the Major Leagues, regrouped into such categories as left-handed starters and leading hitters against left-handed pitchers. James also made up whole new methods of combining statistics using formulas and simple algorithms such as "Basic Runs Created Formula," and "Isolated Power," all seeking to compare specific strengths and weaknesses of individual players using

Sabermetrics—the empirical analysis of baseball statistics. This concept of statistical analysis may not sound strange to us today with the growth of online sports gambling and fantasy sports leagues, but it was in in the late seventies and early eighties. While Bill James may have been popular to academics like my father and his cronies and was without question the basis for Billy Beane's success with the Oakland A's in the nineties, the subject did not attain pop culture significance until Michael Lewis wrote *Moneyball,* which Brad Pitt and Jonah Hill brought to life on the silver screen.

Baseball is a sport awash in statistics, and this appealed to the statistician Bill James, my scientist father, the baseball man Billy Beane, and the author Michael Lewis. It is not, however, just the statistics that appeal, it is how statistical analysis and position play can inform decision making and predict an outcome, whether for a major league or fantasy team, or for any organization. On our team, we all have different strengths. The extroverts enjoy project management, whereas the introverts enjoy their time designing and drafting. When we are working at our best and most collaboratively, each member of our team gets to practice in the areas they excel but also to learn and grow in the areas in which they may be weaker. The sum of the parts creates a better whole, and together we can put up a great win-loss record.

# Tone Check

Politicians, business owners, and everyone working in hospitality or retail understand success stems directly from "connecting" with their audience. Children are taught to say please and thank you, to look people in the eye, and to smile. Most of us at DFA are effective communicators, having honed our social skills long before working here. In addition to these natural skills, we have become fluent with technology-aided communication, especially email. Without question, email increases efficiency, provides a 24/7 platform, and when properly managed, provides a searchable archive of communications and decisions. While we enjoy all the benefits, we also spend a great deal of time training ourselves on how to best optimize email.

To help appreciate the challenges and opportunities presented by today's technologies, it helps to understand our evolution over the last three decades. In 1991, when we embarked on our adventure, we had a conference room, beepers, and phones, but fax machines were yet to arrive. Drawings were done by hand, and conference room tables and job sites were the meeting places of choice. Cell phones, desktop computers, tablets, smart phones, and email were science fiction. We were given our first personal computer, a Mac Plus, in 1992—about the time we started loading thermal paper into our first fax machine. Beepers, pay phones, and calling cards may only be vaguely familiar today, but until 1993 or 1994, this was how we stayed in touch when urgent matters arose. As each new technology was introduced, we inched forward, wondering how we had been productive prior to the new, new thing.

Now we have Google and iPhones, and email has become our primary professional communication tool; with the cloud available to store a seemingly infinite amount of material, project correspondence is archivable and accessible. Relationships are no longer cemented solely by looking people in the eye or by the quality of a handshake. We speak or email with one consultant near daily, and I realized recently that only a few of us have met the consultant face to face. While digital correspondence enables efficiency, email presents meaningful new challenges. Not only are the foundational tools of syntax, grammar, and spelling subject to reinterpretation, conveying meaning and managing tone is made difficult without personal interaction. Reading and writing is much harder and time consuming for people than spoken conversation.

If you wander through our office, you will hear periodic requests for a "tone check." Frequently, we find ourselves in an email dialogue with a client, contractor, or consultant,and a draft response has been composed. How will the email be received? Does the email seek to blame, rather than to solve? Will the email fully answer the posed question, or will it occasion further confusion? Are the appropriate parties, and only the appropriate parties, copied?

Once sent, an email becomes part of the record, and more "tempests in a teapot" have been created by firing off something hasty, nasty, or ill-considered

While we work hard every day to control the tone of that which leaves our office, we also work on accurately interpreting the tone of incoming emails. It takes patience to forgive the implicit and often explicit tone of emails. Correspondence is often not checked for tone before its author hits send, so we endeavor to forgive an author who writes—and sends— before thinking, and we aim to read emails in the best possible light. Perhaps someday, professional email will evolve into a correspondence tool that can stand on its own, yet I perceive a lessening of standards, rather than a trend toward greater care and manners. It's too easy to be ill-considered and hasty; and now that texting, Twitter, and Instagram are dominating social correspondence, taking care with email might seem quaint or unimportant. While I don't expect people to follow my lead in writing grammatically correct texts and relying less on emojis, our process of tone-checking emails will remain in place here at the office.

.

# Yes, And...

Our most important ideas are often borrowed wholesale. Several years ago, I heard Tina Fey speaking about a comedic improvisation concept titled "Yes, and…" To paraphrase the insanely smart crew from Second City in Chicago, an improv sketch dies as soon as someone says "no." Regardless of how uproarious a statement in a skit may be, the improv actor's response must only be an affirmative "yes!" and "yes" must immediately be followed by the conjunction "and…" or the skit dies.

The team at Second City realized this concept applies to more than improvisation and started offering business seminars and published a book setting forth the principles of "Yes, and…" (*Yes, And; How Improvisation Reverses "No, But" Thinking and Improves Creativity and Collaboration – Lessons from Second City*, Kelly Leonard and Tom Norton, 2015). I share the belief that the philosophy applies to many human endeavors, and especially to the creative process and project management aspects of residential architecture. If you were to ask my children which word their father likes least, they would respond resoundingly with "no." "Yes, and…" would not be the first business concept I've taken home at the end of a week.

What we find so compelling about "Yes, and…," is that the concept applies equally to both the creative and project management components of our practice. When a contracting partner says, "no, we can't do that," our office is trained to say immediately, "Yes, and…," meaning "what might we do instead?" When a client prefers a design solution that seems less optimal than other propositions, we get to a better answer by understanding their point of view and then moving the conversation forward. Disputes dematerialize as soon as we apply "Yes, and..." approach.

One Monday morning we were talking about "Yes, and..." and going a bit deeper, I stipulated that the concept applies most particularly to unexpected discoveries during construction. Once the shock wears off, unexpected discoveries present unexpected opportunities. Coincidently, we heard the same day from a contractor that demolition had uncovered surprises at a site, and that the open plan we designed could not be accomplished. Reminded of the morning's talk, the project team dug in and found solutions in response to the bad news, and the final design was unanimously preferred over the original design.

More recently, a different contractor informed our office that we had failed to issue a late revision to an appliance schedule, resulting in the wrong wine refrigerator being ordered and installed—another interesting test case for "Yes, and..." The contractor's first reaction was, "too bad, the client can live with it," especially given the difference was solely aesthetic. We could either accept that nothing could be done, or we could accept responsibility for the mistake and find a solution; replace the door on the unit or swap out the unit and cover a punitive restocking charge. Returning and restocking the unit proved to be the best answer, and covering the accordant fees returned a meaningful dividend. By admitting/affirming the mistake ("yes") and finding a solution ("and..."), we demonstrated that we are both professional and accountable, and our relationship with our client improved rather than deteriorated. We certainly don't look to make mistakes, but when we do, "Yes, and..." is an indispensable tool.

When presenting a "Yes, and..." response to a tough situation, people are often skeptical or think we are just trying to "spin" the situation. It is has been proven, however, that "Yes, and..." is a sincere and disciplined system of thought that provides us with a collaborative and affirmative framework to resolve conflicts, overcome mistakes, and exploit opportunities.

Thank you Tina Fey for bringing the concept to light and to The Second City for sharing its tool kit.

# "I Didn't Mean To"

We get a lot right, and we also make mistakes. Others do as well. This means much of our time is spent discovering errors, tracing history, and finding solutions when not making amends. The navigation of mistake assessment and mitigation follows a predictable path.

As soon as something goes wrong, everyone's first reaction is usually a self-protecting hope that the mistake is not their own. This hope is universal as an initial reaction, and while usually unspoken, and somewhat embarrassing, it has little to do with understanding or addressing a purported error. Research is required to find out the veracity of the error, and then immediately upon confirmation, to assess the impact of the mistake. Eventually, the conversation will move on to accountability.

Historically, our professional insurance was referred to as malpractice insurance. The word "malpractice" skews towards negligence and, even, malfeasance. Accordingly, we now refer to our insurance as an "errors and omissions" policy. As an old friend of mine once said, mistakes take two forms: those of commission and those of omission. Both types share attributes, they occur either through misunderstanding or miscommunication.

Once a mistake has been identified, the first requirement is to determine whether the incident is fairly characterized as an error. Many mistakes turn out to be miscommunications with one party not fully understanding the steps along the way to successful implementation. We are frequently called to a job site to review a crisis, only to find that the crisis is really just due to partial completion or based on poorly visualized or partially understood design intent. It's always a relief when the mistake turns out to be nothing of the sort.

When mistakes are not misunderstandings but are objectively errors, two paths need to be traveled. The first path is aptly defined by the children's book *Beautiful Oops* (Barney Saltzberg, 2010), wherein the author demonstrates how to make beauty from blobs of spilled ink, ripped pages, and cross-outs. Certain architectural issues are surprises and sometimes they cannot be changed and need to be embraced ("Columns are Our Friends"). Finding that mistakes are not mistakes at all, and finding exciting new design possibilities are happy outcomes to otherwise tense situations. As for teaching a methodology, all I can offer is patience and thoughtfulness, personality traits that tend to run for the hills when crises come for a visit.

Patience and thoughtfulness also serve us well when black-and-white mistakes arise. On every project, conflicting client needs and desires push us in different directions. Pages and pages of drawings need to be coordinated, the work product of engineers and consultants require integration with the architectural plans, and hundreds of materials and products require specification. It is fair to say that we have never completed a project without a mistake in one of these areas, and it is statistically improbable to think we will complete a project without making several bone-headed, avoidable, and inconvenient mistakes. Appliance model numbers change or get inaccurately transcribed. Given the complexity of the documents we produce, it is easy to imagine a critical dimension being mistyped, and typos can have a large impact. The computer has made our day-to-day more efficient… and easier to propagate false information, a danger of cut-and-paste.

Other stakeholders make mistakes as well. Contractors do, as do consultants and engineers, and even our clients offer conflicting direction. Part of our daily job is to attribute mistakes to the account of the appropriate party. As we go through this process of assessing responsibility, we believe that architects should enjoy no more of a free pass than contractors, consultants, and clients. Ownership of mistakes and investing in relationships pays dividends. Covering a restocking fee due to an inaccurate specification or reimbursing a contractor to change the swing of a door is a small price to pay, and demonstrates a sincere commitment to the concepts of partnership, responsibility and accountability.

Having a varied playbook for assessing and resolving situations is essential to any business, particularly so for architects. While assessment and mitigation efforts allow projects to move forward, we also need to address the emotional landscape surrounding mistakes. People are invariably angry with those who make mistakes; even when affirmative solutions are found, nerves can fray and relationships can falter. This is particularly true for associates who have made mistakes, especially those which can be characterized as sloppy or careless. All too often an associate will say to me a version of "I didn't mean to." I recognize this is a shorthand version of an apology, but for me it misses the mark. I can't think of any associate during my career who intended to make a mistake, especially an inconvenient, expensive, or avoidable one. Such behavior would be insubordinate, or worse.

Even when a matter is resolved, certain situations warrant an apology, and that should be the end of it; unless, of course, a promise is made to take more care in the future – which is helpful, no matter how hard it is to accomplish.

# Solutions, Not Blame

Problems cross our desk every day. Some are caught ahead of time, whereas others only emerge as work is performed on site. When problems occur, it is human nature for each stakeholder to explain why the problem is not of his/her creation and to point a finger at the perceived culprit or culprits. The challenge is that the accused is usually equally prepared to point a finger at someone else, even the accuser. On this path, dispute resolution can become more tiresome and expensive than simply solving the problem. We use many methods to understand and determine responsibility, especially when project costs and schedules are escalating, and to seek opportunities to improve collaboration and get a struggling project back on track. One of my favorite techniques is to gather the project team in a circle and to ask each member why the project is running behind schedule. Giving each team member a limited, but uninterrupted, time to speak to the delays, it is predictable that each member will describe in the gentlest words possible why the delays are the responsibility of each of the others. After each team member has spoken, I often surprise the group by stating that, if each story were accurate, we must not by definition be behind schedule. Once the snickers and quizzical looks subside, I recommend we share the responsibility, and learn how to better work in support of each other.

With enough practice, the distributed blame and forward-looking attitude satisfactorily puts contractors and subcontractors at ease. The more difficult situations to resolve are those that stem from specific mistakes attributable to individuals, whether created by clients, contractors, subcontractors, consultants, or our own team. Responses to this category of issues range from denial to apology, neither of which are particularly helpful. In these situations, careful study and attribution of responsibility for mistakes is essential, especially when costs are involved. Defining responsibility is not a solution onto itself. The calmer head, the one we like to bring to every situation, defines the path of solutions, not blame.

As we seek solutions, we aim to close the responsibility issue. Once it is clear who made a mistake, it is much easier to move towards resolution. Lingering over the circumstances makes no one feel better, nor does it help the resolution. Invariably, the person at fault feels relieved at getting the issue in the rearview mirror. Once responsibility has been determined and any economic resolution approved, we can study solutions. Similar to the forthright process of assessing and understanding the problem, the swift proposition of solutions is mandatory to the reestablishment of positive momentum. As we go though the solution seeking process, the very best outcome is for the person at fault to propose the solution. There is no quicker way to go from doghouse to hero than accepting responsibility and then saying "what if?"

# Urgency, Not Haste

A careful study of the time, quality, and money equilibrium would suggest that an over focus on urgency may have a net negative effect on a project. Urgency pushed to its end becomes haste and leads to mistakes, sacrificing quality and design considerations, likely costing money through unnecessary corrective work. But that is just a clinical argument. More significantly, haste disrupts the creative process. A rush to finish solely to meet the demands of a client, boss, building, rules and regulations, or contractors, often produces substandard results.

We tuned in to a Ted Talk by Adam Grant on "Original Thinkers," and I am pleased to report that successful residential architects may be the perfect blend of "*pre*-crastinators" and "procrastinators." Many of our best ideas and solutions come at times when we are not specifically focused on the specific task at hand. For me, I all too often wake up at four in the morning with an idea, mull one over in the shower, or while walking to work. Slowing down and letting ideas percolate is not necessarily a sign of laziness or a lack of drive; sometimes it's the most direct route to the best answer.

Deep in thought one morning on the subway, I got off one stop later than usual. My walk to the office was a few minutes longer, providing me a little extra time for my thoughts as I ambled along.

For many years, I have said that my hope is to have one good idea a day, just one. For me, and I am certain for others, these good ideas—

whether small or big - come at unusual moments. Frequently, they arrive somewhat unexpectedly in the middle of a meeting, surrounded by people and triggered by a comment or by a drawing seen in a new light—a "Eureka!" moment. The intensity of design meetings cannot be understated, and for this reason, I find them incredibly enjoyable. This is the exhibitionist, performance side of my personality, in full display when deliberations and new ideas come fast. Countless projects have materially benefited from a single idea blurted out during a design meeting.

We also perform our best work at other times, at moments when we slow down, unplug, and allow our minds to wander. On the subway, walking around the city, in the shower, or half-asleep at four in the morning. Inspiration frequently comes when our mental processors are running at half-speed or in background mode. With the constant barrage of emails, phone calls, and meetings, daydreaming is no easy feat and takes discipline. Often, we can only accomplish this form of distracted focus by mistake, by skipping a stop on the subway, having our smartphone battery die, or by insomnia. I've found it's very challenging to schedule time to unplug, unwind, and to let my mind wander, even though the benefits are so obvious.

Note: July 17, 2018. Soon after writing the above installment, a friend came to visit and brought me a book: *Thank You for Being Late: an Optimist's Guide to Thriving in an Age of Accelerations* by Thomas Friedman (2016). After reading just a few pages of the first chapter, I was reminded of lessons learned many years ago; no ideas occur in a vacuum, and insights come to people when unexpected free time appears. I am impressed that as a professional journalist he can continue with his thoughts for 453 pages – I look forward to reading them all. As for that week's Monday morning meeting, I very much enjoyed quoting from the early chapters. It beats tying my remarks to another sports or movie reference.

# Herb Cohen was Right, Mostly

In 1980, my "retired" parents opened a bookstore in our adopted hometown of Grand Rapids, Michigan. Their decision to open the store was a very personal one. I know they loved books, they seemed to have read most, if not all of them, but wouldn't that occasion someone to visit a library or the mall or some other bookseller? They didn't need to open a bookstore. They might have continued their teaching careers. They might have stared down the barrels of more microscopes, or they might have simply stayed at home and led girl-scout troops and coached Little League teams. But they didn't, they would prefer to live in a city with an independent bookstore and to be a cog in a recovering downtown's bustling main street. Their personal decision was anchored by their sense of civic duty and cultural leadership. As an adolescent, I had mixed feelings about this bookselling endeavor. My parents were academic, and book-learning is a long way from cool. My parents weren't cool, at least not in the eyes of a teen obsessed with competitive sports and making friends.

Having one's parents own a bookstore wasn't always great fun. I was expected to work when I might have preferred to play, and the continuing education aspect was very difficult to appreciate as a teen. Reflecting on it now, I can't think of a route to a better education than coming of age as a bookseller's kid. One of the perks of owning a bookstore was hosting authors who were traveling the country on book tours. Given that our bookstore was in Grand Rapids, Michigan, this meant we were not likely to be visited by best-selling authors like Pat Conroy or Stephen King. Yet, two particular authors you have probably never heard of made quite an impression on me, and are in fact, the only two I can specifically recall. I still possess the original volumes of each author some forty years later.

The first was Joe Girard, who wrote a book titled *How to Sell Yourself* (1979). At the time, Mr. Girard held the *Guinness Book of World Records* title for selling the most cars in a single year. His writing has not stayed with me the way Hemingway, Fitzgerald, or Auster's have, but I've never forgotten a story he told about a lost sale. By recollection, a woman came into the showroom and after considerable deliberation, kicking the tires so to speak, she settled on a model. While executing all of the customary paperwork, she became nervous and thought to have a cigarette. Confronting an empty pack, she asked Joe if she could have one of his. Unfortunately for the completion of the sale, Joe did not smoke the same brand. The woman excused herself, jumped in her jalopy, promising to be right back, and drove off to replenish her supply. Apocryphally, she never returned. Joe Girard's response was to go to the store himself and to buy one pack of every popular brand, and never to lose another sale that way.

The second author was Herb Cohen who had just penned a similar self-help book about negotiation, *You Can Negotiate Anything* (1980). I recall a number of stories from Mr. Cohen's book, and recently I read the tome again to refresh my memory. I frequently borrow stories from his book; even after so many years, I occasionally recommend the book to friends and colleagues. My favorite memory of Cohen was his opinion that "if you don't miss a plane, train, or bus once in a while, you are spending too much time in airports, train stations and bus stations." I rely on this for my just-in-time but relaxed approach to getting to the airport. Unfortunately, one Friday, Cohen's aphorism came rushing back to me as I missed an early morning flight. While Herb Cohen might have applauded the fact that I had missed a flight, the third during a life of travel, I think the reason for the snafu would have infuriated him. I arrived forty minutes before my flight, and the skycap told me it was too close to departure to accept my checked bag, not surprisingly, golf clubs. After going inside the terminal and getting rejected by both a self-check-in kiosk and an airline representative, it became clear that the airline had introduced a forty-five-minute preflight deadline, which could not be overridden. While I was disappointed to miss the flight, I had no one to blame but myself. If I had left my apartment promptly at 5:30 a.m. as intended, rather than dawdling a bit, I would certainly have made the flight. Standing in line at the help desk instead of waiting at the gate to board, I began to wonder whether Herb Cohen might be right about missing a flight once in a while, even if not based on the narrow rationale of saving time for other important business needs. Instead of being angry at a stupid rule or even with myself, I wondered if I could take advantage of having an unplanned two hour break from rushing about (see Thomas Friedman's *Thank You for Being Late*).

After getting rebooked, I went through security. Since I was no longer in a hurry, I did not particularly mind that my TSA PreCheck status was not marked on my boarding pass. The line wasn't too terribly long, and it wasn't too inconvenient to slip off my loafers and take my laptop out of my briefcase. Holding back my frustration, I wandered out to my gate, and my eyes alit upon one of the ubiquitous terminal retail spas with its rows of massage chairs fronting the concourse. I had two hours to kill, and it was 6:52 a.m., not really five o'clock anywhere. I walked a little further into the store where I met a salesperson at the register with another customer. I unplugged and sat down for a thirty-minute chair massage, just as so many other travelers have done before. This gave me some time to think: to think about how long it had been since I had a massage; to think about how easy it is to be upset, and how hard it is to overcome inconvenience or frustration; to think about and remember my parents; to look forward to seeing some of my dearest friends; and how, even so, I would miss my family over the weekend. Mostly, I tried to think about nothing and to enjoy the success my masseuse was having at kneading away my stress. After the chair massage and paying the tab, I chatted for a bit with the masseuse about his background and his work. I like to think he was pleased to have someone show an interest. After settling the tab and bidding adieu, I sat in one of the mechanical massage chairs and thought some more, deciding to write this story.

And then it was 8:00 a.m., the hour the concourse bar opens—definitely five o'clock somewhere. I ordered a Bloody Mary, emailed my friends to tell them I would join them on the back-nine, opened my computer and began to write. I don't believe Herb Cohen would ever have taken such pleasure in a missed flight, but I still credit him with teaching me an easy attitude when it comes to travel and the bumps along the way. At the end of the day, Herb Cohen was right, mostly.

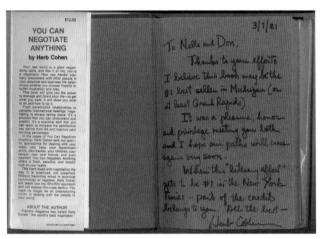

*Inscription by Herb Cohen to my parents, Nelle and Don.*

# Charette

When I first began the study of architecture at Harvard GSD's Career Discovery Program during the summer of 1982, our drafting and model supply store was named Charrette. Eighteen years earlier, the first Charrette store was opened by two graduates of the Harvard Graduate School of Design who had trouble sourcing supplies as students. The chain eventually grew to a total of eleven retail stores located throughout the United States. When I moved to New York to study at Columbia (1998-1991), the Charrette store was on Lexington Avenue in the thirties, and we often made the trip downtown to purchase supplies. CAD began to replace hand drafting in the mid-nineties, and the big box office supply stores made Charrette's retail business less sustainable. By 1997, the business was imperiled and investors swooped in. Stores were shuttered and while an effort was made to establish an online footprint that eventually failed. Sadly, the charrette.com domain name is now available for purchase, something I could not have imagined while I was a student. If I were to ask around the office, few of the architectural staff will likely remember the store, nor would they feel nostalgic for the velum, mylar, and Koh-i-Noor Rapidograph pen sets, or even for Charrette's orange Helvetica logo so fixed in my memory. But they all know what it means to be "on charrette," and every once in a while, I have the opportunity to remind them.

The etymology of being *en charrette* dates to the 1880s at the Ecole des

Beaux-Arts in Paris. When assignments were due, the proctors would wheel a cart (*charrette*) through the studio collecting the students' drawings and models. According to lore, one or more students would invariably hop on the cart—*en charrette*—as it was wheeled by, putting the finishing touches on their drawings or models. When pulling all-nighters in the studio at the end of each semester, architecture students frequently boast to their non-architecture school friends, that they were "on charrette," as if being on charrette was code for inclusion in a sleep-deprived secret society. I recall the on-charrette rite of passage as a defining part of my architecture school education, and I think these memories are shared by most, if not all of my colleagues.

Even though we fondly recall the glory days of school and tell tall tales of days and weeks of sleepless nights and dozing though reviews, I've done everything in my power to keep the *en charrette* concept from our office. When we started the firm, we chose to differentiate ourselves from firms that demanded "interns" work eighty-hour weeks. During the years immediately following graduate school, one of my closest friends worked for the late Charles Gwathmey. Taking a day off on the weekend to ride the subway to Van Cortlandt Park to play golf was a bridge too far. For me, the baffling thing was that my friend was so happy in his job. He was working on great projects with equally dedicated colleagues, and the excitement of the job overcame any sense of exploitation. As I tell him to this day, "good for him, but not on my watch."

As we say, "rules are meant to be broken," and periodically, we will undertake an in-house *charrette*. On one occasion, we realized two small and very technical projects were overdue and were getting pushed aside by other projects. We had missed deadline after deadline and were beginning to feel as if the design and construction documents might never be completed. So I pitched the idea of a three-day *charrette*. All hands would put aside other work, as best as possible, and work together to finish the document sets for the two projects. I would buy lunches and pour wine, and we would work with the energy and enthusiasm we all recall from our student days. The plan was well received and the *charrette* went smoothly, and the studio was abuzz at 10 p.m. and later. Occasionally, it is fun to break the rules and rise to a challenge. It's also fun to repeat a rite of passage, as long as it does not become habitual.

# Hot Potato

Most high-functioning executive skills track back to children's games, in this case, hot potato, the game where a "hot" potato is passed back and forth until the music stops—exactly like musical chairs, but less aerobic. The object is to be not left holding the potato, a perfect analog to the process of collaboration at the heart of residential design. When working with clients, consultants, and contractors, drawings and specifications are traded back and forth at a constant rate with much of the dialog revolving around who is waiting for whom. Who has the potato? After our Monday morning meeting, we often sit together and field the many questions that inevitably have come to us over the preceding weekend, deciding who should reply to each specific inquiry.

Architects seek perfection, and in its pursuit, become hesitant to publish partial information or to prematurely issue documents. Undeniably, we become frustrated by the all too frequent ninety-percent decisions proffered by our clients, by the incomplete submittals by contractors, and by the oft-lagging work by consultants. We often forget that "perfect is the enemy of good," and we, too, withhold our work product. Seeking to perfect our work, we wait until emails are tone-checked, until documents are edited, coordinated, and complete, and that we are comfortable with what we are communicating. While this careful approach avoids mistakes and epitomizes professionalism, it can also materially hinder efficiency. Every day, we work on passing the "potato" and overcoming our professional desire to hold our cards close. Productive collaboration comes from forthright communication, even when transparency may create vulnerability. Balancing professionalism with a willingness to share in-process work is a constant yet rewarding challenge.

Whenever I feel overwhelmed, I make to-do lists. I can't help myself. Most of my lists have become catalogs of tasks for others to complete, and while this may annoy or even embarrass my team, it demonstrates how to pass the potato. How can I touch a piece of paper only once? How can we make our processes more efficient through better communication and sharing our work product at incremental stages rather than waiting for wholesale completeness? All I can offer as an answer is constant encouragement to share, to communicate, and to publish.

# ENGAGEMENT

DF 1986

# Bubble Chart

Since 1991, my team and I have steadily built a practice, one bubble at time. It has not always been smooth sailing. The Great Recession of 2008-2009 dramatically impacted our business. New commissions were few and far between, project budgets were scaled back, and our revenue faltered. Still, we fared better than most. We had not over-expanded during the preceding boom, and we weathered the storm.

Despite its many challenges, the recession came with a silver lining: we had time for reflection and self-assessment, the benefits of which have endured. During those dark days, we started two analytic projects. The first was a database of construction costs for completed projects. We also collected data on change orders and the resulting cost increases, whether based on scope creep or site conditions discovered after the commencement of construction. This information, distilled and updated over time, positively influences every aspect of the firm.

Our second analytic endeavor was to create a genealogy chart of sorts, visually documenting the historical connections between our projects and clients. What might we learn if we went back to 1991 and diagrammed which projects came from which? The task was cumbersome, but after a few false starts and software swaps, we developed our Bubble Chart, a graphic constellation documenting each referral and connecting the dots between them (see page 1).

We've learned many things from our chart:

1. Malcolm Gladwell is right: "Connectors" really do exist.

2. Relationships matter. Ninety percent of our projects are either for repeat clients or for new clients that come to us through direct referrals.

3. Sharing the Bubble Chart with new clients both reassures and burnishes our reputation. It demonstrates that we have more at stake with their project than just its immediate outcome, as a bad report has a ripple effect.

4. Small-town economics work in the largest city in America. Word-of-mouth and community are as valuable in New York as anywhere, maybe more so.

Most importantly, we recognize that our Bubble Chart is our greatest asset. It is a daily reminder of who we are, how we got here, and where we are headed. It inspires us to stay in touch with our friends and former clients, and to shine in our new endeavors as we build our business, bubble by bubble.

# Expecting Expectation Management

If we were to search the Basic Services section of our contracts for the phrase "expectation management," we would come up empty. Our contracts describe our services and establish performance expectations, but they do not stipulate a requirement for managing expectations of others.

On the rare occasion a client is dissatisfied, we might hear with great sincerity that we could have better managed expectations. Is the client really saying we should have lowered expectations for a project; and if we had managed these diminished expectations and met a lowered bar, that the client would have been more pleased with our performance or the outcome? I contend the goal of meeting and exceeding expectations has been unwittingly replaced by a lesser request of managing expectations. We keep report cards on projects, and similar to our contracts, we do not have a "managed expectations" review category—our grading occurs exclusively along the scale of performance and whether we met expectations, not how well we managed, or manipulated, expectations.

This does not mean our partners don't demand and deserve expectation management. It's the language of our time, and clients need a framework at the onset of a project as to how things are predicted to unfold, and they often rate our management of their expectations just as sincerely as actual performance. In response, we work as professionals to diligently set, refine, and exceed expectations. Walking through project responsibilities and sharing our time- quality-money triangle helps, as does carefully coupling budgets and scope. Quality baselines, programming, and attainable goals lead to meeting or exceeding expectations through performance.

While over-promising and underperforming damages relationships and reputations, the opposite course of underpromising and overdelivering by way of expectation management is a fundamentally deflating approach for creative endeavors. The answer, therefore, is simple. Communicate clearly, perform well, meet and exceed achievable goals; in turn, have fewer unmet expectations to be managed.

# Accommodation or Encouragement

We enthusiastically practice and teach "Yes, and…;" our borrowed guide to everyday interaction, which we conjoin with a "customer is always right" bias. While these affirmative strategies form the bedrock of a successful professional practice, they do not apply to every situation nor do they define every relationship.

Collaborating on the design and construction of a private residence is an emotionally and economically charged exercise for everyone involved. Architects, contractors, and clients each hold varied opinions about the process and the details, and these opinions may conflict. When agendas start to veer and the seeds of distrust appear, the disarming approach of "Yes, and…" usually does the trick. Yet, if agendas, opinions, or personalities diverge too greatly, "Yes, and…" can have an opposite effect. Affirmative strategies only work when parties behave collaboratively and seek solutions not recriminations.

Sometimes, affirmative strategies can lead to over-accommodation. By seeking appeasement and avoiding confrontation, projects can careen down blind alleys as efforts are made to empathetically accept a differing, possibly oppositional or inaccurate point of view. While disarming and well-intentioned as such mollification may be, disingenuous accommodation can easily become encouragement, or worse, indulgence. The upside of accommodation is elasticity and flexibility, which are at the heart of collaboration. The downside is a lack of forthrightness and honesty.

At times, project needs and desires are at odds and cannot be simultaneously satisfied, and criteria and objectives need to be prioritized. While compromises and subtle resolutions are always good first steps when resolving conflicts, parties occasionally dig in, determined to pursue individual agendas or just simply to win arguments at any cost. When this occurs, affirmative strategies can backfire and become counterproductive.

In 2017 and 2018, we had a contractor who repeatedly refused to produce revised construction schedules, and when pressed, submitted schedules that were both inaccurate and misleading. Our client joined us in collectively working with the contractor, rather than demanding performance or terminating the relationship. Unintentionally, the contractor's misguided belief that they could reach the finish line with only minor improvements to their management and performance was reinforced. Unfortunately, the schedule issues were symptomatic of diseased project management, and every accommodation distracted us from harsher measures that may have in the end been wiser.

In addition to underperforming contractors, third parties—decorators and consultants, for instance—may also fail to deliver complete or timely information essential to move forward with an aspect of a project. Instead of confrontationally demanding completion of the subject task, architects and contractors invariably seek workarounds. While supportive and collaborative, this type of flexibility and accommodation encourages further poor performance, amplifies mistakes, and results in increased costs and schedule extensions.

The exact same problems stem from client indecision. Hesitant to commit to choices that are difficult to change, clients quite often keep options open until the last minute and provide direction with only ninety-percent commitment. Architects, designers, and contractors all too often hesitate to press the client for final answers. Accepting by accommodation the ninety-percent decision reinforces the opposite of that which is needed—a final 100% decision.

# Attitude

When interviewing a potential contractor, a wise client asked a disarming question, "What qualities would make us good clients?"

The contractor, not wishing to appear presumptuous, and perhaps fearing a trick, paused thoughtfully. Before he could answer, one spouse began to speak of the clients' mutually decisive personalities, letting the contractor off the hook by answering on his behalf. The contractor, in turn, built upon the clients' self-assessment by confirming the importance of making decisions before construction commencement, indeed a very sound recommendation. After listening for a bit, I interjected with a simple thought. One trait could singularly describe the very best clients, "attitude."

This attitude is, of course, a positive attitude. Commissioning a custom home is a rare event undertaken by very few, and the stresses that come with the process are appreciated only by the same few. Many clients, especially first-time clients, approach the design and construction process with fear and even dread. This hesitation comes from a reasonably educated expectation that their dreams will cost three times the budget and be delivered in double the allotted time. Accordingly, the informed client comes to us with their antennae up, ready to fight to protect their interest against the casino run by the egotistic architect and the opportunistic contractor. Even when a project runs smoothly, budgets and schedules may still dramatically inflate, causing tensions to surge. Unanticipated conditions and late-stage additions invariably arise during construction that further the delta between budgeted and actual. Maintaining a positive attitude when project schedules and budgets slip can become extremely challenging, especially when a culture of blame erodes the collaborative spirit.

While the actual responsibility for maintaining schedule and budget lies with the general contractor, the architect directs the movie and manages the team. Along with designing, drawing plans, and preparing specifications, the architect's job is to set the tone for a project. This cheerleading of sorts is most notably needed when additional work expense and schedule extensions threaten to infect a project that began as exciting and rewarding. Helping all parties maintain a high level of confidence in the team, the process, and the project outcome ensures that clients enjoy the process and make good decisions along the way.

There is a wonderful parable about the empty or full glass that goes something like this. Pessimists find a glass half-empty; optimists find a glass half-full; and the engineer finds the glass twice as large as it needs to be. I am happy to be an architect, not an engineer. Electing to measure the glass as half-full suits my vision, and I encourage others to join me in maintaining a positive attitude - no matter how tightly their jaws may be clenched.

# Curtain Emergencies

In the early 2000s, we collaborated on an apartment renovation project with a now-famous interior designer. Over the course of the project, the designer and I became friendly and when catching up by phone one Monday morning, I asked how his weekend had been. He told me with some noticeable glee that he had just fired a client. I asked him to elaborate, and he said he had received a call from his client over the weekend asking for an immediate callback—the subject matter being a "curtain emergency." When he finally returned the call on Monday morning, he pushed back, stating that "unless said curtains were on (insert expletive) fire, there was nothing he could imagine that would qualify as a "curtain emergency." After confirming that the client's house had, indeed, not burned to the ground, he confessed that he'd chosen to become a decorator to celebrate the fun and style in life, and that the client might find someone better suited for her needs.

I recall exactly where I was when I had my own "curtain emergency." I was standing on the first tee of a golf course in Hot Springs, Virginia, about to commence an afternoon round at an annual outing. My phone rang: the office was calling. Everyone at the office knew I was unreachable except in the case of an emergency, but should something truly important come up, to please call. We had just finished an apartment renovation on the Upper East Side and the interiors were being installed in my absence. The associate on the call was in a panic; there was blood on the very expensive just-delivered off-white Holly Hunt sofa. At first, I thought the office was playing a practical joke, but when I realized the panic was real, I reeled off a couple of quick questions. Was the person who was bleeding still bleeding and was the injury severe? Was the bleeding individual still proximal to the sofa? Once it was established that no one was badly hurt and that no more blood would be spilled, I asked my colleague to call Fiber Seal, a company that treats upholstery, and to ask them whether the stain should be cleaned while wet or dry and by whom—our team or professionals)? Within minutes, we knew that the blood should be cleaned once dried and that hydrogen peroxide would remove the blood without damaging the sofa, and I returned to my pre-shot routine. Even had the damage been worse, was the situation really any different than a garden variety "curtain emergency"?

We take our work seriously, and often find ourselves solving problems and settling matters of meaningful consequence. Project schedules and budgets are real and leave little room for creative interpretation. Building systems need to work without compromise. Client happiness with the finished product is paramount and troubleshooting is a big part of what we do every day. Our entire business is founded on the quality of service we provide and upon the reputation we enjoy.

Notwithstanding, we can all take things a bit too seriously from time to time, elevating minor issues to calamity status. A punch-list item is less important than a systemic shortcoming. Paint colors can be adjusted through repainting; leaks require the opening of walls. Our foremost priority is to get the walls right, as well as that which is behind the walls. Fine-tuning may make the difference between glee and exorbitant glee, and while perfection may be the goal, we strive to not let "perfection become the enemy of good."

# Yeah, I Know a Guy

Loiter around construction sites, and you will invariably hear a response of "yeah, I know a guy." Successful contractors always know whom to call to get something done, especially when a task demands expertise beyond the skills of the field team. Calling upon such resources is akin to a general practitioner recommending a patient to a specialist, and these referrals are no more than a doctor's affirmation of "yeah, I know a guy." I find I've adopted the saying, so much so, that my every utterance of the phrase elicits snickers and eye rolls from my colleagues.

Other than "thanks, guys" or "come on, guys," the colloquial has largely receded from general usage, and nowadays, that "guy" may not be a guy at all. Sometimes, she's a gal, and sometimes he or she is a cardiologist, professional engineer, or consultant who would be offended at being labeled as such. Regardless of gender, age, education, or expertise, having personnel resources beyond one's own team is extremely valuable. As a residential architect in New York City, one of the first "guys" one gets to know is an expeditor, a consultant who can navigate the bureaucracy of the Manhattan and Brooklyn divisions of the NYC Department of Buildings—and just as importantly—the NYC Landmarks Preservation Commission. For the past twenty years, our guy is both a guy named Walter and a gal named Jackie who, together with their team of assistants, attend to all manner of incomprehensible and always-changing DOB issues. When municipal approvals languish, clients invariably ask "what do expeditors do?" Many times, I reply "you have no idea," and frankly, sometimes, I don't really seem to know. Notwithstanding this sophomoric attempt at humor, I am acutely aware that the bureaucratic DOB approval process would be even more Byzantine and inefficient if not for our close relationship with our expediting team.

In addition to our expeditors, we work with engineering consultants on a near-daily basis. Engineers speak in tongues, and communication between engineers and architects is made challenging by opaque technical jargon. This private language takes a long time to master and building trust between architects and engineers requires commitment from both sides. We've partnered with our mechanical and structural engineers for more than twenty years each and whenever we find ourselves in a pinch, I can make a call and cut through the noise and get a much-needed answer. With our structural engineer, more than with any of our consultants, we enjoy an especially personal and intimate relationship. Our guy's name is Edy, and I refer to him as my self-selected godparent. When I am really in a pickle and need someone to lead me to safety, I call Edy. Several decades ago, Edy was the lead engineer at one of the largest architectural and engineering firms in New York City and on his fiftieth birthday, he resigned to start his own firm. Today he employs friends and family and has become a referral-based leader specializing in New York City façade repair and restoration. He and his firm work predominantly with building owners, building mangers, and commercial architects, servicing much larger interests than those of our smaller-scale residential work. In fact, we are the only residential firm with whom Edy works and, even more importantly, the only firm, large or small, with whom Edy socializes. When our team finds a structural problem particularly confusing or challenging, Edy and Adam, his hand-picked successor, will drop by the office and hold class while we ply them with food and drink. To have unlimited access to engineers of such intelligence and experience makes us much better at everything we do.

The importance of knowing a guy came naturally to me, even before I knew to place such weighty value on knowing a guy. Soon after founding the firm, I met a man named Hugo Ramirez. Before he retired, Hugo was New York City's preeminent expert, collector, and restorer of pre-electric lighting, operating out of a small and overstuffed shop and workroom on East 59th Street. The store, which he called a gallery, was about a 1,000 square feet and was surrounded by similar looking shops selling similar looking lighting, except those shops were not similar at all. Hugo's fixtures were museum quality, in either original condition or professionally restored by Hugo himself.

I don't recall exactly how I met Hugo—he didn't advertise—but for about ten years, he was a very special guy to me who shared his great love and knowledge of antique lighting. Hugo was more than a bit mercurial and hard to get to know and to this day; I am astonished by the extraordinary access and friendship Hugo offered me. I recall he was very pleased to have worked with the set designers of *Amistad*, and that he was just as pleased to have tossed out the folks from *The Age of Innocence*. Evidencing great disdain for the chicanery of others, he elected to restore fixtures for only one antique dealer in town (Hirschl and Adler), and rarely at that. I believe the last piece he restored for a museum was for the grande-dame Metropolitan Museum of Art. He was tickled when his fixture made the cover of the catalogue, even if his days of working for others were numbered. Despite his pride and periodic standoffishness, he had all the time in the world for me and for my colleagues and clients I brought around to his shop. When we would schedule a visit to his gallery, I would tell my colleagues or clients to budget at least two hours so Hugo could take us through the entre history of pre-electric lighting, and one-by-one go through his collection of rare and significant and now-electrified fixtures. On a good day, he would turn off all the lights in the shop and illuminate a single fixture, demonstrating how significant the light from a single lamp would have been in a period without today's abundance of electric lighting. His stories and examples of factory finishes, whale oil and kerosene fixtures, argands, sinumbras, and gasoliers fascinated me, and he was equally energized by my interest. As the trust between us grew, Hugo would patiently share his great love of lighting, as well as the methods by which other less honest dealers ruined fixtures, stripped factory finishes to raw brass and overcharged for reproductions or undocumented fakes.

Fast-forward to present day, I continue to make new friends with areas of expertise otherwise unfamiliar to me. In the same way that Hugo welcomed me to his gallery decades ago, Darius Nemati does the same whenever I am in the market for a rug, or even just when I yearn to lose a few hours going to Long Island City for a little continuing education in something truly authentic. Darius was introduced to the rug trade at birth. His father, an émigré form Iran, brought with him to Manhattan in the 1970s an unrivaled knowledge gained from family collections and having witnessed the weaving of rugs on family lands.

Darius continues this tradition out of the former Scalamandre Silk factory building in Long Island City and spending an afternoon "flipping rugs" with Darius and his team is as restorative as my visits with Hugo used to be. In 2022, when Darius was at our house for a visit, I let it slip that I really should replace my indoor-outdoor rug in our great room. An ember from the fireplace had burnt a small hole in it, and while it had been bought to withstand stains, which it didn't do well, it was drab and tread worn. A few months later Darius invited me to his loft to see a few carpets. He had brought in five rugs for me to review, all contemporary and right sized. At some point, I asked what might have been an embarrassing question, would it burn as easily as the synthetic rug we were replacing? Without saying a word his friend and employee Sany, who may be one of the best re-weavers and restorers in the States, took a blow torch to the back of the carpet—the exact carpet that is now the foundational design element in our great room.

From the essential engineer to experts in subsets of the decorative arts, our projects are more successful, and our lives enriched by the guys and gals we know. I realize I know and enjoy working with people in just about every field of endeavor; fellow architects, designers, and educators; bankers and insurance brokers; building superintendents, teachers, writers, editors, and publishers; hardware and plumbing fixture sellers; website developers, car mechanics, and vintage boat guys; pinball enthusiasts, booksellers, bartenders, and maître d's; and even artists. We are thrilled to know the artists whose efforts we promote, collect, and hang on our walls.

I've learned that getting to know a guy takes investment, an investment in time and most importantly, curiosity. Every guy and gal I've come to know, and upon whom I've come to rely, I've gotten to know through mutual interest and genuine appreciation. When I say "yeah, I know a guy," I say so with confidence this architect is likely that same guy in return.

# Zip-Coding

Our office is headquartered in Midtown Manhattan and a majority of our projects are private residences here on the island. A quick perusal of the Sunday *New York Times* Real Estate section highlights how expensive homeownership is in Manhattan, and with internet search engines providing an easy method of tracking publicly recorded sales histories, the wealth of our patrons cannot be concealed. Expensive real estate acquisitions are accompanied by high-quality expectations in both design and construction. Taken together with stringent municipal and building requirements, only the best and most qualified professionals and contractors are offered jobs in certain zip codes. We take great pride excelling in this competitive market.

No matter the locale or how much capital is available for construction, homeowners frequently feel projects are simply too expensive, often incomprehensibly so. Even clients who are well prepared to receive bids feel compelled to challenge the numbers. One explanation is that construction costs correlate to a specific market. We refer to this as "zip-coding," a conceptual framework that costs are dramatically affected by a client's affluence, a specific project address, and by the value of the real estate. Construction costs vary by location, but not as much as the variability of the underlying real estate in different zip codes. And the very affluent locales validate the high costs of custom home design and construction.

Naturally, project costs vary based on location. It is more expensive to build in Manhattan than in other communities due to regulatory concerns, limited work hours, traffic, insurance costs, labor costs, gratuities; all of which are legitimate overhead costs. The same is true and even more so on Nantucket and Martha's Vineyard, in the Hamptons, and in resorts like Aspen and Palm Beach. To make certain construction costs, no matter how high, stay connected to the market forces of supply-and-demand, and not become unduly inflated based on project location or perceptions of a client's wealth, we use several strategies to manage costs and deliver value.

The first core strategy is to develop close long-term relationships with contractors, and in turn, subcontractors, who manage their overhead costs carefully, have a high quality-to-value track record, and are less prone to opportunistically inflating costs. We split our portfolio of contracting firms into tiers and try to match the caliber of the contractor to the project. While we occasionally work with the more expensive firms who have exceptional resources with correspondingly higher overhead rates, most of our projects are placed with smaller, more efficient firms with lower overhead and project delivery expenses.

The second strategy is to work closely with our clients to help them understand which scope elements of a project may be elective, and to offer guidance when a less expensive design solution may satisfy their needs. While we love beautiful and expensive things, we often propose alternate materials that we like as much or more than more costly options. We have found contractors are willing to work collaboratively to reduce expenses when clients demonstrate financial discipline.

The DFA STUDIO Program represents our third strategy. The program is a prix-fixe and pre-priced design and construction program based on our most popular design elements—our greatest hits. The program was conceived as a response to runaway costs due to many factors including zip-coding and scope creep. To create the program, we collected pricing data from our completed projects. We then went to our contracting partners to get a sense of how much might be saved if we were to decrease the number of selections available to a client, especially post construction commencement. The DFA STUDIO Program has been able to deliver projects at an average discount of twenty-five percent, when compared to our Custom Commissions—and at an average change order rate of only two percent.

All three strategies reinforce our fiercely held belief that sound fiscal management is in the long-term interest of our clients and construction partners. By giving clients better financial control of their projects, we increase the trust between all parties—enhancing rather than diminishing design quality. These strategies are particularly useful when working in the most expensive zip codes in the country.

# Houston, We Have a (PR) Problem

During the spring of 2019, I read a Facebook post from a summer acquaintance, self-admittedly ranting about her New York City apartment renovation and the extended schedule that was occasioning her to skip travel plans for her son's spring break, as she had to stay home to manage the conclusion of the project. What surprised me was that the subject of her animus was not her Park Avenue building's work hours, mercurial board, or even her general contractor. The post placed the blame squarely upon her architect. Intrigued, I read the seventeen comments that had been posted.

The comments poured gasoline on the fire, with the most astounding comment stating without humor that "most architects do this since they couldn't hack it as used car salesmen." A second startling comment recommended the client should not "pay for one change order!" The owner gently refuted this recommendation, stating that the project's budget control was quite good, and that change orders were negligible. The all too frequent allegation assumes that architects create change orders and encourage out-of-line pricing without an understanding of the project metrics. For the record, it is unusual for an architect or general contractor to benefit from a schedule extension or cost escalation. In this case, it sounds like there were no meaningful additional fees attributable to runaway change orders or scope creep. The third response was specific to the particular architect who was familiar to the person commenting on the post. The allegation assailed the architect for being a "GC's architect"—as are most by implication—and not an effective agent of the owner, which is supposed to be the architect's primary role. Notwithstanding the inaccuracy of the agency premise, the widely held belief that architects sell out and are incented to assist general contractors in an effort to increase costs and inflate fees is absurd. No architect could operate an ongoing business within a community or ever have a repeat client if such an assignation were true.

Projects don't always go perfectly. Architects can certainly contribute to delays through poor communication or design disagreements—and even through mistakes—but this venomous social media rebuke of our profession was particularly naked and slanderous. While I have no insight as to whether the project's architect performed well or poorly, or if unusual circumstances contributed to delays, I find the broad character assassination of our shared profession truly sobering. My DFA family and many of my colleagues have spent a career confronting such sentiments through enlightened and fair professional practice, and our repeat clients and the friends we have made on all sides of the business tell us we have succeeded.

Yes Houston, we have a (public relations) problem, and it may be more endemic than I might ever have realized.

# Après Ski

Since day one, our practice has been based on relationships, and I've found no better way of establishing new friendships than through sports.

I moved to Manhattan directly after graduating from college, with few acquaintances and no disposable wealth. Given this lack of friends and funds, the prospect of enjoying a Hamptons summer share was remote. I did, however, have Central Park and a pair of soccer flats. That first summer, and then the next, I spent five or six hours each Saturday and Sunday playing pick-up soccer on the grassless Great Lawn with a rag-tag group of Europeans, Latin Americans and Middle Easterners. Many days I was the only (North) American, learning to appreciate diversity and inclusion from the vantage point of a minority, and earning my way onto the pitch through quality touches and good humor. That my nickname was "Gringo" amuses me still. A few years later I picked up with an organized team sponsored by a small French restaurant. After each game we would decamp to Tout va Bien on the famed Restaurant Row for country pâté, sausages, and vin rouge. Our most talented player was a then recent transplant from Marseille who had played in the First Division and spoke barely a word of English, a perfect match to my lack of French. Yet, we got along famously on the field, and when he and a partner decided to open a bistro in SoHo, I became their architect. Designing my first restaurant in Manhattan was exciting; wining and dining with the ex-pats after hours perhaps even more so. On this very French team—many of us smoked cigarettes at halftime—our right wing was the lone other (North) American. He was a few years older than I and unlike most of the waiters, barbacks, and busboys that filled the other positions, he was a Stanford educated partner at a Midtown law firm. Off the field, he became a mentor and role model, demonstrating how to balance a career, family and even sports; he also became an early client of the firm. Although neither of us still play competitively, we stay in touch and have remained friends for thirty-plus years.

I'll always be an unwavering fan of team sports, even though continued participation has been hampered by age, family time, and weekends in the country. Playing soccer at midnight at Chelsea piers with young bankers or at dawn in Riverside Park with a group called the Geezers— yes, I've done both—holds less appeal every year. Fortunately, I found a different outlet by joining a social club near our office that has one of the foremost squash programs in the country. For twenty-five years, I've played regularly and have made great friends, the closest since college. Not incidentally, our bubble chart of clients boasts many accomplished squash players, and both my social and professional lives are infinitely richer for the friends made on court.

In spring, summer, and fall, I now mostly play golf and tennis. While appalling, the age-old adage that playing "golf is good for business" still rings true. I often play with clients and contractors and walking the links has strengthened relationships with both. Golf's tradition that rules violations are the player's responsibility prioritizes sportsmanship. The game can reveal an opponent's character and at the same time, provide a snapshot of one's own. If an opponent were a bad sport—golfers are known to cheat on occasion—how would he or she be as a client? If I were similarly charged, how would I perform as their architect?

Sports need not be competitive to be effective in building relationships, which brings me to the title of this installment, après ski = sports marketing. I loved skiing as a kid, and occasionally thereafter, all the way through graduate school when I tore my ACL during a winter break.

I had the surgery, suffered through the rehab and, full of excuses like hating the cold and skiing's inconvenience and expense, I racked my skis and took a twenty-five-year hiatus. When my kids were young, I again buckled my boots, and we now count skiing among our favorite activities, both close to home and afar. Our winter calendars are built around skiing. Most weekends you can find us at a small hill in the neighboring town of Cornwall, Connecticut, and each spring break we travel to Lech, Austria, a family vacation that the kids even prefer over a return trip to Disney World.

While I have come back to enjoy skiing as an adult, I fully admit to being a bluebird participant, and if the weather isn't perfect, I have no hesitation spending my time in the lodge or at the spa. I recall a particular Connecticut weekend when rain failed to turn to snow, and while this didn't bother the kids, I left my gear at home. Waiting in the lodge as the kids got soaked in ski school, I ran into three other sets of parents, one for whom we had renovated their city apartment and designed their CT home; the second for whom we had just broken ground on a new house near ours; and the third, a friend for whom we were just beginning to discuss designing their home. A few weeks later, at an après ski party, at a home we had designed, I was introduced to yet another potential client. Until then, I had thought nothing could beat soccer, squash, and golf for making friends and developing relationships. I now feel skiing may give them both a downhill run for their money. Let it snow, Let it snow, Let it snow.

# Lunch

I go out to lunch as often as possible. Even to me, my penchant for working lunches seems out of another era: part *Mad Men*, part 21 Club, and part Irish bar. Reading that last line, the lunches I describe might come across as both pretentious and limited to middle aged white men with drinking problems. As it turns out, my dining companions rarely fit these stereotypes.

The first group I like to take to lunch is comprised of members of my team. I enjoy their company, and I love continuing our conversations about both general subjects and specific projects while out of the office and relaxing at lunch. In smaller groups and between bites, we dig a little deeper, and we can address sensitive subjects without worrying about eavesdroppers—the diners at adjacent tables don't often take much interest in our conversations. I also remember the firm where I worked between college and graduate schools. The principals were mentors and great bosses and are friends to this day, but they did not socialize with their staff. Perhaps such walls are good for business, but for my money—and I do pick up the check—our culture is at least in part built on going to lunch, birthday parties, and frequent happy hours.

The second community of stakeholders with whom we dine with is made up of our contracting partners. When we go out with our builders, we accomplish many things. Foremost, we break down the expected hierarchy by treating our contractors as partners, not adversaries. The amount of goodwill we've built by having a meal and a bottle of wine with our builders cannot be overstated. Beyond good will, we solve, or at least attempt to solve, specific project issues as well as the industry challenges we all confront.

Most business owners would put our third category of lunch companions first. Accountants used to call client lunches entertainment. Lunches with clients can certainly be entertaining, but the real value is in the opportunity for frank communication. Much of what we do is nuanced and is better communicated face-to-face, and talking over a meal amplifies this opportunity. If you want to actively discuss ideas, which would you prefer: email or sharing a meal?

And lastly, something I do frequently, I like to go out to lunch by myself. Dining alone provides precious downtime and an opportunity to recharge. I always remember to bring my notepad to jot down my meandering thoughts.

# WINDING DOWN

*DFA Team t-shirt art for the 2019*
*Neew York Architects' Regatta Challenge*

# Architectural Scales

Since entering the workforce, albeit self-employed, I've looked back on my education with curiosity. I was extremely fortunate to have been admitted to some of the best schools in the country and made it to graduation at each of the schools in which I enrolled, even when my academic performance was subpar. Each school I attended took me deeper into the theoretical and further from that which I would spend my career practicing. The academic offerings of my Master of Architecture program at Columbia University could not have been further from my vocational education in mechanical drawing class at East Grand Rapids Senior High School. Thirty plus years after graduating from Columbia, I am convinced this is exactly as it should be, a realization that only came recently.

For many, many years, I felt our most competitive architectural schools had become woefully deficient in teaching useful skills which post-graduates would need when they entered the work force. During the pandemic, we hired a computer-proficient young woman who had received a Bachelor of Science in Architecture from the University of Virginia, the same degree I received from the same school in 1987. She did not know how to use an architectural scale (a triangular ruler with not so cryptic markings representing different architectural scales such as 1/8", 1/4", etc.). I suppose my father might have felt similarly when my pocket calculator replaced his slide rule for calculations that could not be figured in one's head. As someone who has hired and trained many recent graduates, I am in a natural position to judge a candidate's practical education obtained prior to arrival at our firm, and my anecdotal rankings of programs and institutions seem to be the inverse of the reputations of the most elite institutions. Columbia, the last institution to confer upon me a degree, held a very special place at the top of my least respected list, followed closely by Princeton, Harvard, the rest of the Ivy League, and a school in Los Angeles named SCI-Arc (Southern California Institute of Technology). I generally give Yale a free pass, as their school of architecture seems sincere in its efforts to teach pragmatic skills and architectural history. To be fair, during the era in which I attended Columbia, the teaching of architecture in the United States was undergoing a paradigm shift away from professional practice toward research, theory, and the studying of architecture at scales well beyond triangular pieces of plastic or aluminum with archaic markings.

This gulf between professional practice and the academy placed a boulder-sized chip on my shoulder. This chip was my companion until several conversations with professors and colleagues in preparation for returning to my alma mater as a visiting critic. While the chasm is no less wide, I've come to understand and appreciate the drivers behind the education evolution at our top architecture schools. The schools compete for the best and brightest students, and today's students are not seeking a vocational education. Graduate schools are particularly keen on challenging students to analyze the world and reimagine it, and on a scale for which there are few job postings for entry-level positions. This work that students undertake is much more exciting, and in many ways more valuable than the classical training obtained by previous generations. When schools compete for the best students, they are really competing with one another, and once Harvard, Columbia, and Princeton changed direction, the rest of the top schools followed suit. As a middle-aged residential architect, I try to think of this shift in educational priorities from vocational to theory as a generational gap and not a referendum on the profession.

Architectural education was a continuum from the founding of the Ecole des Beaux Arts in 1648 through the early 1990s. Architecture was a profession, no different than engineering, law, and accounting; architectural students were trained in the art and science of making buildings. When I was an undergraduate student at UVA, we still learned watercolor techniques, how to construct two-point perspectives by hand, a certain amount of building technology and engineering, and the history of architecture and design from antiquity through 20th century modernism. It was something of a grand tour of architectural education, geared toward a career in the field. When working with students today, I am fascinated to see that beyond their sketchbooks, these subjects seemed largely unfamiliar. Computers have replaced drafting tables throughout the design studios, and 3-D printers and laser cutters have largely reduced the prominence of bass wood piles, chipboard scraps, and unfinished and discarded model sections. The studio landscape in school mirrors the large-scale architectural offices in big cities that dominate professional practice today.

The change in teaching methodology is not limited to technology advancements. The subject matter has also changed, as architecture is no longer limited to the design of human-scaled buildings, Vitruvius be damned. Students are taught to think on a grand and global scale, and to reimagine how we might build. These explorations are aided by new technology, as theoretical projects such as these could not be conceived, developed, or rendered without the awesome power of computers.

These systemic changes were codified for me in the fall of 2023 when I traveled to Venice, Italy and Charlottesville, Virginia, as a visiting critic with the UVA Architecture School's study abroad programs. In Charlottesville, I met with a second-year graduate student who voiced an interest in residential architecture and who lamented that the only prerequisite professional practice class will be taught in the second semester of his final (third) year. He also noted that the class does not teach a form of professional practice with which I would be familiar. Our conversation reminded me of a brief chat I had as a student with Daniel Liebeskind when he came to Columbia as a guest critic. After a presentation on the Holocaust Museum then under construction, I asked him whether he thought the days of a residential practitioner—a "gentleman architect" I recall saying—was possible. His dystopian and dispiriting reply—to me—was that he felt such a career path was over, dead, and buried, and never to come back (paraphrased). This was one of many inspirational moments at graduate school that kickstarted the founding of our firm doing precisely what the wise master said couldn't be done. The next time I ran into Liebeskind was after a talk he gave at the Harvard Club soon after winning the competition to design the Freedom Tower. I was invited by the host committee and at dinner afterwards, I asked Daniel's wife Nina whether they had selected an architect to help with their New York City apartment renovations I had heard they were contemplating. They had retained someone else, but it did confirm my belief that architectural practice happens at very different scales and that even someone gifted enough to design the city's tallest skyscraper would be wise to hire a very different type of architect to design and oversee an apartment renovation.

As I have gone back to teach, I've had the opportunity to engage with other teachers and practitioners of different stripes and different scales. While the trend has been towards globalism, theory, urban planning, and social issues, I have been gratified that a growing minority of students pine for exposure to architecture practiced at a smaller scale. Every year, we offer to host a student extern from UVA, and in 2023 we had a record fourteen students apply.

I believe Daniel Liebeskind's design was the best competition entry for the Freedom Tower, and I am glad that our schools bring the "Starchitects" back to teach and to inspire. Even so, he was wrong when it comes to the plausibility of an old-fashioned small town residential practice being able to succeed in this era. We come to work every day in the shadows of Billionaire's' Row, to a townhouse office that feels like a home, and with a team that feels more like family than staff. We design homes one at a time for an ever-expanding roster of enthusiastic clients. And yes, we still use pen and paper and make models by hand.

# DFA House

The DFA HOUSE is a semi-pre-fab modular home concept that we have been developing since before the pandemic. It all started over lunch with a dear friend in 2017. He told me the story of a lake in the Highlands of New Jersey that he and his sister own. He told of how his grandfather and brothers bought a couple thousand acres and established a fishing camp on the shores of a small lake. They divided the lakeside lots into roughly 100 parcels and leased the lots to friends and fishing afficionados. The first generation built small cabins that were frequently passed down to heirs, along with the remaining years of the ground leases. Over the years, many of the structures fell into disrepair, and the rent revenue was not sufficient to maintain the roads and the dam, and the tenants and my friends had come to legal loggerheads. By the time we had lunch, the siblings and their tenants had resolved their lawsuits, and fifteen to twenty of the lots had reverted to family ownership. At lunch, my friend spoke lyrically and optimistically about their plans to bring the lake back to their ancestors' vision and that they were hoping to build lakeside cottages on the properties they owned, starting with two or three in the next year or so.

And then he shared their architectural vision, homes made from salvaged and repurposed shipping containers. I was gobsmacked, as industrial detritus scattered around the shores could not be more oppositional to the vision of lake and community restoration so romantically described. To make sure I had read this all accurately, I asked if I could join for a

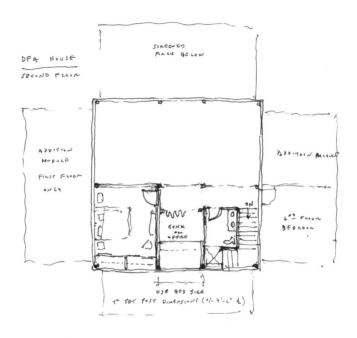

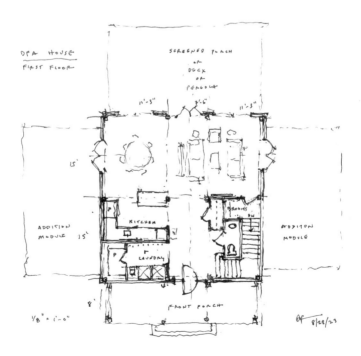

day trip the next time they were scheduled to visit. A few weeks later, we drove out to the lake and then met with the town building officials about the project. During the subsequent lunch, I recommended they abandon the shipping container concept and to let my team take a shot at designing a repeatable cottage for them. Just like any project, we started with programming and eventually fleshed out a concept that featured a simple salt-box volume with a timber frame great room and an efficient mechanical footprint. Unfortunately, the various contractors we asked to bid did not seem to agree that the homes could be built less expensively than our portfolio of custom homes. Either we had been zip-coded, we were not communicating well, or we hadn't found the right answer. Without a contracting partner and not willing to start a pre-fab house company, the project was set aside.

We had spent several months designing an ideal cottage, and another several months trying to realize these early designs. Inertia set in, and then the COVID-19 pandemic hit and explorations ceased. When our team came back after the lockdowns and discussed our future goals, we decided to continue to explore. We renamed the project the DFA HOUSE and started over. New plans were drawn, the timber frame was simplified, and butter board models were built; just like any other project—except we were now designing without a specific client in mind. We are now selling the vision to clients, really to anyone who thinks the efficiencies gained by a pre-designed structure might satisfy their needs. Four years after we started design work for a lake in New Jersey, we were sitting around the office looking at the model on the table and noticed, almost casually, that the DFA HOUSE footprint was still too large. We started over again.

As we go forward, we have many people watching closely. The current version of the DFA HOUSE is conceived as a Certified Passive House and will be an attainable house in that construction costs should be at least twenty-five percent lower than building custom from scratch. Construction timelines should be even more efficient. As we move from prototype to sales, we are considering starting a new company focused only on the development of this singular program, something I could never have envisioned when I first had lunch with my friend.

# Crawl - Walk - Run; Looking Forward

Sometime prior to the onset of the COVID-19 pandemic, we found ourselves undertaking projects that were unfamiliar. I started writing and thinking I might want to teach. We designed a few products, which after five years are now being produced and will soon be marketed. We also began developing a modular house concept which we have redesigned innumerable times. We are hoping to break ground on our first protype model this year (2024). Having come a long way on each of these initiatives, I admit we had neither timetables nor budgets for the endeavors—no more so than having a business plan in place when we established our company (1991).

We did have a definable methodology, which we have termed, "Crawl – Walk – Run." To be fair, this is stolen pretty much wholesale from the expressions, "you must learn to crawl before you can walk," and "you have to put the horse before the cart." These sounds simple enough as do most of the cliched utterances that tumble from the mouths of capitalists on *Shark Tank*. A single moment of inspiration often sets the course of years of development and refinement, and while the path may twist and turn, I contend that the process is fundamentally linear and something we have trained and practiced throughout our careers as architects. Creative ventures each have an origin myth which provide valuable insight into the creative process.

This essay is part of a book project I started in 2016 after a friend casually recommended that I tell my story. His remark inspired me to trek the next day to the Apple Store and buy my first laptop. The computer's absurdly precise record-keeping tells me the first document, an introduction to the then unwritten book *Looking Forward to Monday Morning* was created at 10:33pm on November 5, 2016, and was saved next on November 16. This first introduction did not make it in the final edit. It would take seven years of effort to write and rewrite, to edit and to have edited for me, and to prepare the manuscript(s) for editorial review at our favorite publishing houses. I am very much looking forward to the printing presses running.

We have also begun exploring product design, a whole new category of endeavor for us. Being a new area, and without expertise, we found ourselves in crawl mode. The gestation period of the plumbing fixtures we have designed goes back the furthest and deepest into my subconscious. I was an intrepid doodler in elementary school. I mortifyingly recall my parents returning home from an early parent teacher conference with the instruction to empty my pockets before sending me to school in the morning. Inclined desks were a natural drag-racing track for cars made of erasers and thumbtacks. Pens could be deconstructed and turned into spitball rifles—when not serving as single-use launchers of the ink refills sent aloft by springs that were meant to advance and retract the ball point. Doodling by comparison was harmless and fortunately, no one ever took away my pencils. Among my favorite things to doodle were interlocking rings following the lines of MC Escher's more complex optical illusions. Much later, it was Venn diagrams and spaces of intersection inspired by Carlo Scarpa and the Olympics. Today, doodles cover my desk blotter, and at some point, I decided three dimensional versions would make interesting faucets—neither overtly traditional nor modern. During the early months of the COVID pandemic, I added context to the doodles with a hand-drawn set of faucet collections and had the office team draw them in CAD. They were put aside until the pandemic broke; until I was introduced by a mutual friend and marketing maven to Bennett Friedman, the owner of AF New York, one of the largest plumbing fixture distributors in the country (thanks, Courtney). We had worked with AF New York over the years, but I had never met Bennett and had no reason to think a single lunch would spur our faucet collection from crawl to walk mode. I now carry polished chrome prototype handles in

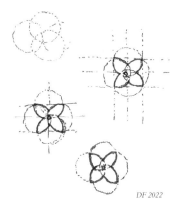

DF 2022

my briefcase. Production is slated for 2024, as are launch parties and then sales. By the time you read this, I am hoping many of our homes will have running water flowing from fixtures of our own design.

Our DFA Fire Chair has enjoyed something of a similar timeline and process to our Line Drawing Faucets. A few years before the pandemic, we were having dinner with friends and after, we sat before a roaring fire in their living room. The modifier "roaring" is often used to describe a post-meal fire in a cozy home, but in this case, "roaring" underserves. It seemed as if there was a wall of fire in their fieldstone fireplace; the logs being stacked higher than basic fire building skills should allow. This was my first time seeing a vertical log holder, a tall grillage of iron that allowed wood to be stacked at the rear of the fire box as opposed to upon a horizontal basket. Inquiries were made and we learned that the log holder was manufactured near our Connecticut home by a company in Torrington, humorously named Grate Wall of Fire. For several seasons, I put a vertical fire grate on my birthday and Christmas lists, but to no avail; it's not the type of item you buy on Amazon or at Bergdorf Goodman. I didn't think too much about it until the pandemic hit and we were spending more time at home and more frequently lighting fires. The Friday before Thanksgiving (2020), I talked my daughter into taking a forty-five-minute drive deep into the country to visit the Grate Wall of Fire store. We arrived at a large steel building in the middle of farmland and strode to the door only to be confronted by a hand-lettered cardboard sign that read "masks NOT required." We dutifully donned our masks, as per the law and our sensibilities, and entered the small storefront. Only weeks before, Trump had lost the election, but this was not clear to the man behind the desk or to the radio talk-show loudly disputing the fact. I turned to my daughter and told her we could leave, but that I did not think we should let politics influence our shopping decisions, and that I really wanted to bring home a vertical fire grate and try it out. Even though we were wearing masks and had arrived in a Subaru, not an F-150, they were happy to sell us a grate. I was most surprised when they gave us a ten percent discount, even though the gentleman behind the counter had not heard of a trade discount. The ensuing civics talk made for a long ride home for my eleven-year-old daughter.

Over the Thanksgiving break, we had many opportunities to show off our new fire-making acumen, and our new purchase performed as we had expected. As innovative as the vertical grate is, however, I began to ponder how it might be even better. I began sketching, which lead to a wholly new patentable design for a hybrid horizontal and vertical log holder, satisfying new aesthetic and performance criteria. Crawling along, we converted the sketches into a model and then began working with a fabricator—who happens to be my old college roommate—to build a prototype. We built two, one for each of us. What had started as an internal competition—surely, I could design a better product than the election deniers in Torrington—took a very positive turn in that our log holder, now called the DFA Fire Chair, performed much better in our fireplace. I felt like Philip Johnson famously bragging about his Glass House in New Canaan and that he just wanted to prove he could design a better house than Mies had for Farnsworth.

Setting aside the origin story and politics, our Fire Chair neither resembles nor performs anything like its horizontal basket and vertical grate predecessors. While ours similarly allows the fire to be built at the rear of the firebox—encouraging smoke to draw up the chimney and not billow out into the room—our chair has a horizontal section that holds the logs off the floor. Raising the logs off the firebox floor creates better convection, essential when starting a fire. The horizontal tines and space below provide for the establishment of a significant ember bed, burning hotter and cleaner than any log holder we have tried. A hotter and cleaner fire also reduces the particulate discharge into the environment and diminishes the likelihood of creosote build-up in the chimney. The shallow second tier—the higher step—allows for building fires in a teepee form, bringing the fire towards the center of the firebox and allowing for a higher fire than can be accomplished by merely stacking wood. The vertical bars facing the room restrain logs from lurching into the room and once the fire is roaring along, logs can be tossed into the fireplace similarly to a wood stove. The demonstrated performance benefits were speculative when making the initial design sketches, but our commitment never wavered in seeking performance gains. We also created an aesthetic departure from Victorian forged iron with a sleek modern work of art in the abstracted form of a seated human figure.

As we moved from crawl to walk mode, we were able to test and retest, and to make small tweaks to the design—improving on the engineering, fabrication methods, aesthetics, and durability—and as to apply for a design patent with the United States patent office. We also produced our first run of twenty Fire Chairs and sold them to friends and family for their enjoyment and as further proof of concept. This first edition sold out almost immediately and twenty new pieces, including eight of a smaller size, quickly followed. And like the faucets, we are looking forward to hitting our stride, including having been selected to exhibit at the 2024 International Contemporary Furniture Fair (ICFF) at the Javits Center.

Reflecting on this burst of creative activity over the past seven years, we realize that this crawl-walk-run process is very similar to the design process we undertake with every home we design. We start with programming and then move on to schematic design, design development, construction documents, bidding, and finally to construction. We have learned this linear path we describe has many twists and turns—and even backtracking. The creative process is the definition of urgency, not haste, and leaves us looking forward every time.

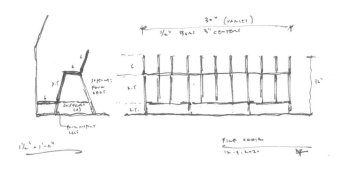

# In Closing

To write this epilogue, I decided to go back to the beginning and to revisit a few significant dates and personal milestones.

Forty-two years ago, as a fifteen-year-old, I picked mechanical drawing as my junior year elective at East Grand Rapids Senior High School. I recall other electives being shop, home economics, typing, and Latin. It was that type of public school that offered both vocational and more elevated learning opportunities. In the spring semester, we worked on one drawing, an exploded axonometric drawing of an object; in my case, a handheld electric razor I had filched from my father's medicine cabinet. My technical drawing "SCHICK ELECTRIC RAZOR drawn by Daniel Frisch, April 23, 1982" is framed and hangs behind my desk along with the entry form and award ribbons from the Detroit News Michigan Industrial Education Awards—Regional 2nd Prize and State 6th Prize. While I am disheartened that shop, mechanical drawing, and home economics are no longer mainstays in most public high schools, I am even more concerned that Latin and the arts have come under attack for funding and relevance considerations—until I get excited all over again now that students learn coding and executive functioning skills.

Nine years later, in the spring of 1991, Columbia University's Graduate School of Architecture, Planning and Preservation conferred upon me a Master of Architecture degree. I had traveled a long distance from Dan Graham's mechanical drawing class where I had dissected and drawn the innards of a razor to earning a professional degree from an elite Ivy

League institution. And yet, as they are meant to be, commencement exercises marked another beginning along a many years journey. A great deal has happened since. I founded a firm, I started a family, and I've written this book of essays about it all.

I first put virtual pen to paper to write an introduction for an intended book in November of 2016; just over seven years ago. I had little more than a concept and a title, *Looking Forward to Monday Morning*, and a format, even though I felt I had at least a book's worth of content rattling around in my brain. I believe I average an hour or so a day of writing (averaged, as I tend to write in bursts without discipline or a repetitive schedule). 365 days times seven years equals 2,555 hours, a little more than a year's labor at an average fifty-hour a week job, but much less than Malcom Gladwell's 10,000 hours of efficient practice needed to become an expert (*Outliers*, 2008). I am certain many more hours will be added to the total before I head out on a book tour or hear from students how much they enjoyed a particular essay.

Taken together, the essays in *Looking Forward to Monday Morning* tell the story of my thirty-plus years of practice; eight times more than the Gladwell minimum. Sending the manuscript(s) on to editors and publishers also offered me the chance to reflect on what to look forward to during the next thirty-three years. As I wrote in "Vocation : Aocation," in the first chapter of this compendium, and I as have tried to affirm in each essay, I feel exceptionally fortunate—both looking back and looking forward—that my vocation and avocation are indeed one.

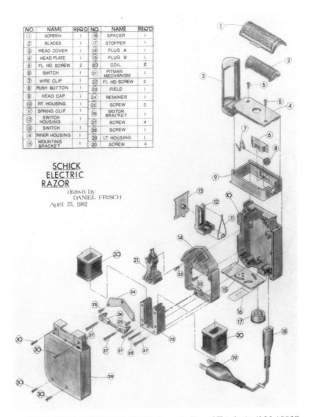

"SCHICK ELECTRIC RAZOR drawn by Daniel Frisch April 23,1982"

# APPENDIX

DF Sketchbook 2023

# Trigger Words

We have created an in-house glossary of "trigger words." When we hear them, we smile as if hearing an inside joke. For your enjoyment, here's our running list:

"**No.**" Everyone in my life, especially my two adorable children, knows this little word raises the hair on my neck. While we cherish argument and spirited discourse, "No" does little to build consensus.

"**But.**" Another little word, similar to "No." If you've been reading these essays, you can easily understand how "Yes, and..." is preferable to "Yes, but..." "But" is a contraction we try to replace with "And" whenever possible.

"**Unequivocal.**" I remember studying for the SAT in high school and one of the tricks we were taught was to challenge the veracity of questions or statements featuring the word "Always." Today our trigger word is "Unequivocal." When we hear of an unequivocal recommendation, we know to equivocate.

"**No problem.**" When we hear this, especially from our contracting partners, our ears perk up, and we think we may, indeed, have a problem. "No problem, it will happen first thing tomorrow." Really? Or, as Danny Meyer, says in *Setting the Table*, "No problem" is no substitute for "You are welcome" as a response to "Thank you."

"**Change order.**" If we were to ask most clients what was most challenging during their project, I would expect to hear "Change orders" near the top of the list. Nothing puts owners and contractors at odds more quickly than late or inflated change orders. Notwithstanding, most change orders are based on additional work or unforeseen circumstances, rather than changes, and change orders are reviewed for appropriateness by our office before being approved, so change orders should not be so confrontational. We've worked with many of our contracting partners for several years and we are finally making headway at replacing the subject line of their paperwork to read "Additional Work Authorization" rather than "Change Order."

**"I mean you no disrespect,"** and **"Respectfully..."** While not unequivocally true, when someone attempts to soften a blow with either of these introductions, we are prepared for an opinion wildly divergent from our own, and my guess is the next statement will not be offered up respectfully. We consider the "respect" intro as nothing more than a little white lie clueing us into a low regard for our position.

**"To be honest..."** See "I mean you no disrespect," and "respectfully...."

**"Constructive criticism."** Usually prefaced with "May I give you a little....," We've found little to be constructive in such offers. Such invitations usually trigger our own form of response: "So noted."

**"I strongly disagree."** A number of years ago, an associate, a client, and I were all discussing the cost effectiveness and cost benefit of a specific floating counter detail and after a spirited debate, the client and I voted for the simpler, more durable, and less costly detail. Our frustrated associate, blowing off some steam blurted out, "But... I strongly disagree." Adding such emphasis did nothing to sway or change the asked and answered decision, and most importantly, did not reflect well on our young associate—although the statement has provided us a quote from our own archives on par with similar lines from *A Few Good Men*.

**"Impossible."** Just another challenge to overcome.

**"Asshole."** It's ok to curse, especially around construction sites, but we do try our best to keep salty language out of emails.

**"I didn't mean to…"** Luckily, people who intend to make mistakes are largely unknown to us.

**"I'm not good at math."** I dedicated an entire essay to this statement uttered too often. I am not particularly good at math, either, but rather than opting out of the conversation, can't we at least try to answer the question?

**"Big boy pants."** When going over the fine points of an office lease in 2016, I was disappointed with a clause setting forth charges to be applied if rent were paid late. Our lawyer recommended I "put on my big boy pants" and pay rent in a timely manner, which was good advice. It amuses me how often we now use the expression when needing to do something we would prefer not to do.

**"One more thing…"** Invariably, these three little words come out as a meeting is breaking. Buckle your seatbelts, a whole host of items are about to be introduced. I promise not to do that here.

# Books

It is fair to say I love books, and books of many genres. Several years ago, I decided to study American history by reading presidential biographies—in chronologic order. I stalled at Polk and need to get back to my project, without regressing and reading the newest biography of Washington, Adams, or Jefferson—or for that matter, Lincoln or Teddy Roosevelt. So many new and fantastic books are written every year, it is impossible to keep up: I just keep filling my shelves.

I grew up surrounded by books. Both of my parents were academics and after their retirement, they opened a bookstore. At the time, I was certain my father had read every book in the store, as he would talk books with his customers all day long and rarely did a book seem unfamiliar. When we sold our house, we donated 6,000 books from my parents' collection to a small town public library in Michigan. Comparatively, my library holds fewer volumes, probably less than 1,000, but they are all dear to me. I read in hardcover—not on a tablet—which is vexing when traveling, and have adopted the habit of wrapping each book in its own plastic jacket, just like a lending library. The books in my collection are well organized, from presidents to biography; from general history to contemporary non-fiction and sports; and finally, to contemporary fiction, which is by far, the largest single category. My shelves are full of Michael Connelly, Daniel Silva, John Grisham, and Carl Hiaasen – is there any better entertainment than a little light reading?

When our family moved to our current apartment, I designed custom wall-mounted bookcases for our books, which have become the main decorative element. Books add color and warmth and activate an otherwise awkward and unremarkable space in our home. At DFA, we have a book called *Living with Books* (Alan Powers, 1999), a design book dedicated to rooms where books are the dominant theme. Whether people shelve their books by color, size, subject, or alphabetically, books highlight a homeowner's' personality. Some are messy, some are austere, some (like me) have OCD; whatever their quirks, readers make for good company.

If you are interested in the books that have contributed most to my thoughts and writings, please visit my bibliographic notes.

*Mona Shores-Workman,* Downtown Books (Grand Rapids, MI),
*June 1985, watercolor on paper.*

# It's a Wonderful Life

During our Monday morning meetings, I often use sports metaphors like "playing extra holes" to demonstrate a particular idea like scope creep. When explaining our STUDIO Program, DFA uses the terms "a la carte" and "prix fixe," two clear descriptors lifted straight from restaurant menus. Most often, I use movies—favorite blockbusters, usually—when calling upon cultural references to illustrate a theme. Even though they are often lost on our younger team members, below are some of my most frequently quoted movies:

*It's a Wonderful Life (1946)*

I hadn't heard of the Frank Capra classic *It's a Wonderful Life* until my first year at the University of Virginia. One of the student organizations sponsored showings before Christmas and it seemed as if the entire student population attended this annual rite. I joined the madding crowd, but with little expectation that the film would have a lifelong impact.

The film's simple themes are as relevant today as when I first saw the movie, and as in 1946 when the film first aired.

• Slow and steady wins the race.

• We each affect the lives of many more people than we realize.

• Wealth should be measured not in dollars, but in the quality of friendships.

- A life of principle has more meaning than a life of materialism.
- A small-town life is as rewarding as big city glamour.

I am proud of how our office culture reflects these themes, and especially so of how we bring a small-town sensibility to our big city practice. George Bailey is a pretty fine role model.

*The American President (1995)*

I reference this Rob Reiner film frequently, almost as often as I watch it when it comes on late at night.

The President is the ultimate CEO and the humorous portrayal of the commander-in-chief's difficulty fulfilling the simple task of buying flowers without assistance from his team echoes the process of delegating tasks in any venture—not to avoid the work but to ensure the work gets done right.

Many of the political issues remain priorities today—gun control, global warming, character defamation—, but the line I quote most frequently is Michael Douglas' climax statement, "I was so busy doing my job, that I forgot to do my job." What a lovely reminder to focus on the actual performance of one's job rather than the applause and critiques proffered by others.

There is a second line I often quote: "Has he lied? Has Bob Rumford lied? Other than the fact that I went Stanford, not Harvard, has Bob Rumford lied?" We often feel ourselves unfairly put on the defensive, criticized over trivialities. I quote this line to remind us that, sometimes, the criticism may be factually accurate, even if not relevant to our performance or overall report card.

*When Harry Met Sally (1989)*

Another Rob Reiner Classic.

No last line of a movie better describes the urgency and excitement that comes with the beginning a new venture or a creative endeavor: "I came here tonight because when you realize you want to spend the rest of your life with somebody, you want the rest of your life to start as soon as possible." We feel this way every time we start a project.

*Shawshank Redemption (1994)*

The film's climax is similar to *When Harry Met Sally*, as Red (Morgan Freeman) says on the bus to Mexico to meet Andy (Tim Robbins): "I find I am so excited. I can barely sit still or hold a thought in my head. I think it's the excitement only a free man can feel, a free man at the start of a long journey whose conclusion is uncertain. I hope I can make it across the border. I hope to see my friend and shake his hand. I hope the Pacific is as blue as it has been in my dreams. I hope." We start every project—at least I hope we do—with this sense of excitement and optimism.

A second favorite line is: "Geology is the study of pressure and time. That's all it takes really, pressure and time. That, and a big goddamn poster." In our case, patience, perseverance, hard work, and whole lot of talent and teamwork.

And finally: "Get busy living; or get busy dying."

*Working Girl (1988)*

In collaboration with clients, engineers, consultants, and builders, architects solve complex problems. Very often, the solutions are nuanced and complicated, and a more straightforward solution might be overlooked. Tess (Melanie Griffith), a secretary and the protagonist of *Working Girl*, provides an unexpectedly simple and elegant solution to a baffling problem—how to get a truck unstuck from under an underpass? "Let a little air of the tires."

We rely on the concept of "letting a little air out of the tires" when we feel the complexity of the answer to a problem is blinding us from a simpler and more elegant resolution. K.I.S.S. (Keep It Simple, Stupid).

*Schindler's List (1993)*

This film is more serious and significant than the rest of this catalog of (mostly) romantic comedies, and the absurdity and hubris of any comparison between the extraordinary accomplishments of Oskar Schindler (Liam Neeson) during the Holocaust and our efforts is self-evident. Notwithstanding, Oskar Schindler's statements of accounting and self-assessment—that he could have done more—is a theme that underlies our culture. In our own way, we do make a difference in people's lives and our efforts to grow the business stem directly from our desire to share our efforts with more clients, to have more employees join the firm and enjoy our affirmative culture, and to share these opportunities with the talented contractors, tradesmen, and craftsmen who collaborate on our projects.

Every December, our firm joins one of our favorite contracting teams at their holiday party. The firm employs eighty-plus people, in addition to subcontractors, and the two brothers who own the company invite these multitudes of employees, subcontractors, and their families—around 250 people. At some point late in the evening, one of the brothers invariably puts his arm around my shoulder and somewhat weepily insists I take in the standing room only crowd, and says, "if not for DFA, his employees' jobs would be in question, and while they would probably find other jobs, they are far better-off because of the collaboration of our two firms."

It seems to me, given such positive reinforcement, that there is always a way to do a little more. We make a difference, how we can make even more of one?

*Charlie and the Chocolate Factory (1971)*

I recently read a book titled *Uneasy Street: The Anxiety of Affluence* by Rachel Sherman (2017). I've purchased countless copies for colleagues and it is part of the bibliography of these essays. The book chronicles affluent New York City residents who have undertaken home renovations—clients like those of our firm. The affluent owners Ms. Sherman interviewed all have different comfort levels with their wealth and the book does a wonderful job of defining the nuances of the anxiety that comes with affluence.

For all the academic insight and nuance Ms. Sherman brings to the subject, *Charlie and the Chocolate Factory* does perhaps an even better job portraying entitlement issues. Each of the children touring the Willy Wonka factory exhibits the tragic flaws of narcissism, greed, spoiled-ness, and entitlement. Yet, when Mr. Wonka (Gene Wilder) says to Charlie at the end of the movie, "and, what happens to the boy who gets everything he ever wished for? ...He lived happily ever after." Well, I am that boy, and we strive to make all of our clients, staff, consultants, and contracting partners feel exactly the same.

*The Internship (2013)*

Although not yet considered a classic, I often watch this when it comes on Netflix. In the film, a couple of guys my age—younger, actually—join Google as summer interns. They find they have leadership skills despite being out of touch with technology, the very foundation of Google. In addition to discovering ways they can contribute, they draw out the talents of a group of young people lacking in social skills and self-esteem. While I lack the acting ability and humor of Vince Vaughan and Owen Wilson and our team has a surfeit of social skills and self-esteem, the story resonates with me. It's all about "Googlieness."

*Ferris Bueller's Day Off (1986)*

Folks who hire architects to design their homes often have very nice cars. Could there be any better prototype for a gallery style garage than the glass house for cars in *Ferris Bueller's Day Off?*

*Pretty Woman (1990)*

While *Pretty Woman* earns its place on this list for more reasons than the frequency with which it airs on cable, one scene perfectly speaks to the aspirational side of residential architecture. As directly quoted:

Vivian: Wow! Great view! I bet you can see all the way to the ocean from out here.

Edward: I'll take your word for it. I don't go out there.

Vivian: Why don't you go out there?

Edward: I'm afraid of heights.

Vivian: You are? So how come you rented the penthouse?

Edward: It's the best. I looked all around for penthouses on the first floor, but I can't find one.

And, as a footnote, the film also features Jason Alexander in a supporting role, who famously played George Costanza on Seinfeld. George's alias and alter ego was Art Vandelay, the most famous fictitious sit-com architect of all time.

*Bull Durham (1988)*

Embarrassingly, here's one more rom-com sports movie. While I always enjoy a screening of the film, I was surprised I added it to my list. I did so for two scenes. The first is the scene where Crash (Kevin Costner) bets his teammates, who are on an epic losing streak, that he can cause a rain-out for the next day's game in spite of an otherwise hot and dry forecast. He does so by turning on the ballpark's sprinkler system, bringing some much-needed levity to the slumping ball club. The stakes need not be so high to assert leadership, and with good humor. When the going gets tough, let's find a sprinkler valve and make it rain.

The second scene is set at the pitcher's mound, where the players gather to address a multitude of personal issues seemingly unrelated to getting the next out. While both the solutions and issues are comedic, the scene is a fun reminder that we all have issues, both on the surface and below, and that we are all on the same team.

And a final quote. "I'm Crash Davis, your new catcher, and you just got lesson number one. Don't think. It can only hurt the ball club. Now come inside and I'll buy you a drink."

*The Replacements (2000)*

I'm not sure this particular film would make the list, if not for one line. "Winners always want the ball when the game is on the line." Shortened, of course, to "Winners want the ball." "Winners want the ball" reminds us to be leaders, and in this movie as in life, it is especially true for underdogs.

*Ford v. Ferrari (2019)*

This film would make my list on beauty alone. The cars, for sure, but also the interior architecture of Detroit and Modena. We even had a client ask that we model a dry bar styled after Henry Ford II's office. As for quotes, Carroll Shelby (Matt Damon) has the following exchange with Henry Ford II (Tracy Letts):

Ford: "Give me one reason why I don't fire everyone associated with this abomination, starting with you?"

Shelby: "Well, sir... I was thinking about that very question as I sat out there in your lovely waiting room. As I was sitting there...I watched that little red folder right there... go through four pairs of hands... Before it got to you. 'Course that doesn't include the twenty-two or so other

Ford employees who probably poked at it before it made its way to the nineteenth floor. All due respect, sir, you can't win a race by committee."

I am glad we chose to be architects and not race car designers. We thrive on collaboration.

---

Whether the above films won Academy Awards or not, these movies—and many, many others—are fabulously quotable and useful to us. While we take what we do seriously, it's very helpful to be able to quote a film when we wish to communicate an idea without sanctimony. These movies provide us a familiar pop cultural language with which to tell our story.

*Dan's books.*

# Bibliography / Reading List

Alda, Alan. *If I Understood You, Would I Have This Look on My Face?: My Adventures in the Art and Science of Relating and Communicating.* New York: Random House, 2018.

Carnegie, Dale. *How to Win Friends and Influence People.* New York: Simon and Schuster, 1936.

Carr, Allen. *The Easy Way To Stop Smoking.* London: Arturus Publishing Limited, 1985.

Colt, George Howe. *The Big House: A Century in the Life of an American Summer Home.* New York: Scribner, 2003.

Cohen, Herb. *You Can Negotiate Anything: How to Get What You Want.* New York: Lyle Stuart Inc., 1980.

Dobrow, Larry. *When Advertising Tried Harder: the Sixties, the Golden Age of American Advertising.* Eugene: Friendly Press, 1984.

Ehrlich, Gretel. *The Solace of Open Spaces.* New York: Penguin Books, 1987.

Feiler, Bruce. *The Secrets of Happy Families.* New York: HarperCollins, 2013.

Festinger, Leon. *A Theory of Cognitive Dissonance.* Palo Alto: Stanford University Press, 1962.

Frank, Robert L. *Richistan: a Journey through the 21st Century Wealth Boom and the Lives of the New Rich.* London: Piatkus, 2008.

Friedman, Thomas L. *Thank You for Being Late: an Optimist's Guide to Thriving in Age of Accelerations.* New York: Farrar, Straus and Giroux, 2016.

Frisch, Don and Nelle. *Celebrate the Harvests!: Michigan Farm Markets, Farm Stands, and Harvest Festivals.* Grand Rapids: Wm. B. Eerdmans Pub. Co., 1995.

Gage, Nicholas. *Eleni.* New York: Ballantine Books, 1983.

Gifford, Henry. *Buildings Don't Lie: Better Buildings by Understanding Basic Building Science: (the Movement through Buildings of Heat, Air, Water, Light, Sound, Fire, and Pests): Important Information for Anyone Who Designs, Builds, Owns, Repairs, Works, or Lives in a Building.* New York: Energy Saving Press LLC, 2017.

Girard, Joe. *How to Sell Yourself.* New York: Simon and Schuster, 1979.

Gladwell, Malcolm. *Outliers.* Boston: Little, Brown and Company, 2008.

Gladwell, Malcolm. *Talking to Strangers: What We Should Know About the People We Don't Know.* Boston: Little, Brown and Company, 2019.

Gladwell, Malcolm. *The Tipping Point: How Little Things Can Make a Big Difference.* Boston: Little, Brown and Company, 2000.

Grant, Adam. Originals: *How Non-conformists Change the World.* New York: Viking, 2016.

Hollander, Stuart; Fry, David, & Hollander, Rose. *Saving the Family Cottage: A Guide to Succession Planning for Your Cottage, Cabin, Camp or Vacation Home.* Berkeley: Nolo, 2014.

Housel, Morgan. *The Psychology of Money: Timeless lessons on wealth, greed, and happiness.* Petersfield, UK: Harriman House, 2020.

James, Bill. *The Bill James Baseball Abstract.* New York: Ballantine Books, New York: 1984.

Knight, Phil. *Shoe Dog.* New York: Scribner, 2016

Kotter, John. *Our Iceberg Is Melting: Changing and Succeeding Under Any Conditions.* New York: Penguin Random House, 2016.

Leonard, Kelly, and Tom Yorton. *Yes, and: How Improvisation Reverses "No,*

*But" Thinking and Improves Creativity and Collaboration*. New York: Harper Business, 2015.

Lewis, Michael. *Moneyball*. W.W. Norton, New York: 2003.

Macy, Beth. *Factory Man: How One Furniture Maker Battled Offshoring, Stayed Local – and Helped Save an American Town*. Boston: Little, Brown and Company, 2014.

McCullough, David. *You Are Not Special And Other Encouragements*. New York: Ecco, 2014.

Meyer, Danny. *Setting the Table: the Transforming Power of Hospitality in Business*. Singapore: Marshall Cavendish, 2007.

Newport, Cal. *Slow Productivity: The Lost Art of Accomplishment without Burnout*. New York: Portfolio/Penguin, 2024.

Poundstone, William. *Are You Smart Enough to Work at Google?: Trick Questions, Zen-like Riddles, Insanely Difficult Puzzles, and Other Devious Interviewing Techniques You Need to Know to Get a Job Anywhere in the New Economy*. Boston: Little Brown and Company; 2012.

Powers, Alan. *Living with Books*. London: Octopus Publishing Group Ltd, 1999.

Reisley, Roland. Usonia, *New York: Building a Community with Frank Lloyd Wright*. Princeton: Princeton Architectural Press, 2001.

Rosenman, Joel, et al. *Young Men with Unlimited Capital: the Story of Woodstock*. Austin: Scrivener Press, 1999.

Ryan, James E. *Wait, What?: and Life's Other Essential Questions*. New York: Harper Collins, 2017.

Saltzberg, Barney. *Beautiful Oops*. New York: Workman Publishing, 2010.

Sasse, Ben. *Them: Why We Hate Each Other — and How to Heal*. New York: St. Martin's Press, 2018.

Schwartz, Barry. *The Paradox of Choice: Why More Is Less*. New York: Ecco, 2004.

Schwartz, Nelson D. *The Velvet Rope Economy: How Inequality Became Big Business*. New York: Doubleday, 2020.

# Roads Publishing's 100 Years of Iconic Toys

## 1884 – 1964
Marbles -1884
Meccano – 1901
Teddy Bear – 1902
Crayola – 1903
Kewpie Doll – 1912
Lincoln Logs – 1916
Hornby Trains – 1920
Yo-Yo – 1928
Cap Gun – 1930
Army Men -1938
Lego – 1939
Skipping Rope -1940
Slinky -1943
Silly Putty – 1943
Tonka Truck -1946
Subbueto -1947
Cluedo (Clue) – 1949
Fuzzy Felt -1950
Mr. Potato Head -1952
Play-Doh -1956
Frisbee – 1957
Scalextrix – 1957
Hula Hoop – 1958
Troll Dolls – 1959
Etch A Sketch – 1960
Sophie the Giraffe – 1961
Easy Bake Oven – 1963
Mouse Trap – 1963
G.I. Joe – 1964
Operation – 1964

## 1965-1983
Barrel of Monkeys – 1965
Thunderbirds – 1965
Twister – 1965
Spirograph – 1966
Lite-Brite – 1967
Mini Till – 1968
Space Hopper – 1969
Stickle Bricks – 1969
Pogo Ball – 1969
Nerf – 1969
Styling Head – 1970
Buckaroo – 1970
Mastermind – 1970
Evel Kneivel Stunt Cycle – 1973
Monchhichi – 1974
Playmobil -1974
Stretch Armstrong – 1976
Big Loader Construction Set – 1977
Star Wars – 1977
Cabbage Patch Kids – 1978
Hungry Hungry Hippos – 1978
Cozy Coupe – 1979
Guess Who – 1979
Rubik's Cube – 1980
Fashion Wheel – 1980
Mr. Frosty – 1980
Big Yellow Teapot – 1981
Glo-Worm – 1982
Super Soaker - 1982
Care Bears -1982
Jenga -1983
My Little Pony - 1983

## 1984-2013
Pound Puppies -1984
Transformers - 1984
Keypers  1985
Teddy Ruxpin - 1985
Teenage Mutant
Ninja Turtles 1988
Game Boy - 1989
POGs - 1990
Baby Born - 1991
Dream Phone -1991
Talkboy - 1992
Beanie Babies - 1993
Sky Dancers - 1994
Buzz Lightyear - 1995
Bop It - 1996
Pokemon Cards - 1996
Tamagotchi - 1996
Tickle Me Elmo - 1996
Furby - 1998
Alien Eggs - 1999
Beyblades - 2000
Bratz – 2001
Squinkles - 2010
Minecraft - 2011
Rainbow Loom - 2011
Lottie - 2012
Kinetic Sand - 2013
Frozen Dolls - 2013

# Acknowledgments and Appreciation

Better judgment aside, many people have believed in me. My parents, for sure, no matter how trying those early parent-teacher conferences must have been. So, too, did Keith and Tig; Chuck, Greg, and Roger, and so many others, when I arrived at college more than a little wet behind the ears—and who are still in my corner so many years later.

Here's to my first partners, Edward and Amy, and every associate who has worked at DFA through the years. Here's to Kate, Devon, Kent, Jamie, and Deborah—who have helped lead the team these last ten years (more like thirty for Jamie).

Here's to the admissions committees of the schools who controlled the gates of higher education and saw something in me that my transcripts didn't describe. Here's to my teachers: Dan Graham at East Grand Rapids Senior High; Jim Thule and Ken White at UVA. More recently, thank you to Kim Haggart, Malo Hutson, and Bill Sherman for asking me to come back to teach, and to Theo van Groll for both keeping me in school and helping me find my way back.

Here's to the Valmarana family. To Mario for teaching and mentoring me and to Betty for mentoring and minding Mario. To Francesco and Alex and Boody—and to Stucky, too.

Here's to the friends I made so long ago on the pitch and courts and course. To Marc, John, Bill, Jamie and Phil. To Mark and David, and Tom and Scott.

Here's to the builders. To Gus and Steve and Johnny, to Tad and Wojtek; to Arlen, Kent, and to Vinny. To Jared, Neil, Brad, Randy, Tim, and Eliot. And to Buddy, too. Thank you for making our plans come to life.

And, to my readers. To Charlie Defanti, John Weber, Joel Rosenman, Adam Van Doren, and Alex Birnbaum; and to Tom Casey and Silvia Erskine. To Nancy Bentley and to Greer Levy. To Celia, who not only read and edited but tried to teach me to write.

Here's to Jake Anderson, Brooke Biro, and the team at ORO Editions for making the book better at every turn. And to Courtney for helping bring all we do to a larger audience.

Here's to the clients, classmates, and friends—too numerous to name. None of this happens without you and I raise a glass to every one of you.

And finally, to my family. To Darcy, Nelle, and Buddy. Thanks for putting up with my talking in paragraphs and for sharing—begrudgingly at times—my love of grammar and manners.

*DF 1986*